OUT OF THE INNER CIRCLE

D1508104

OUT OF THE INNER CIRCLE

*The True Story of a Computer Intruder Capable of
Cracking the Nation's Most Secure Computer Systems*

T E M P U S ™

Bill Landreth
(aka "The Cracker")

PUBLISHED BY
Tempus Books of Microsoft Press
A Division of Microsoft Corporation
One Microsoft Way
Redmond, Washington 98052-6399

Library of Congress Cataloging in Publication Data
Landreth, Bill, 1964-
Out of the inner circle.
Includes index.
1. Electronic data processing departments — Security measures.   I. Title.
HF5548.37.L36   1984   658.4'78   84-25402
ISBN 1-55615-223-X

Printed and bound in the United States of America.

3 4 5 6 7 8 9 FGFG 3 2 1 0 9

Distributed to the book trade in Canada by General Publishing Company, Ltd.

The Tempus Books logo is a trademark and Tempus® is a registered trademark of
Microsoft Corporation. Tempus Books is an imprint of Microsoft Press.

UNIX® is a registered trademark of American Telephone and Telegraph Company.
Apple® is a registered trademark of Apple Computer, Inc. Commodore® is a registered
trademark of Commodore Business Machines, Inc. CompuServe® is a registered trademark of CompuServe, Inc. Cray™ is a trademark of Cray Research Incorporated. Nova®
is a registered trademark of Data General Corporation. DIALOG® is a registered service
mark of DIALOG Information Services, Incorporated. DEC®, DECnet®, and VAX® are
registered trademarks and VMS™ is a trademark of Digital Equipment Corporation.
Dow Jones News/Retrieval® is a registered trademark of Dow Jones and Company, Inc.
HP® is a registered trademark of Hewlett-Packard Company. AT®, IBM®, and PC XT®
are registered trademarks of International Business Machines Corporation. Microsoft®
and MS-DOS® are registered trademarks of Microsoft Corporation. Prime® and Primos®
are registered trademarks of Prime Computer, Incorporated. TRS-80® is a registered
trademark of Radio Shack, a division of Tandy Corporation. The Source® is a registered
trademark of Source Telecomputing Corporation.

Disclaimer. Microsoft Press has not undertaken a comprehensive investigation of the facts
and representations of the author with regard to particular computer systems, operating
systems, or other products. Consequently, although it has no knowledge of any inaccuracies
in the author's treatment of particular products, Microsoft Press makes no warranties or
representations regarding their accuracy and disclaims all liability therefor.

20184366 RB
9/11/91

Contents

Foreword

This book tells you about many of the experiences and stories that were part of my life as a sixteen-year-old hacker. I've tried where possible to make references general, rather than specific, to avoid giving you the impression that a particular hacking approach or technique always works on a single type or class of computer system. Hackers try all kinds of things – they have nothing to lose and everything (in their eyes) to gain.

This book gives my view of the hacking experiences I describe. If, in writing, I have misrepresented or misunderstood any event, I have done so unknowingly. As I state many times: Computer security is ultimately the responsibility of the people who use computers, not of the machines and programs themselves.

While a book reflects the feelings and opinions of the person who writes it, there are many other people who commit their time and their abilities to making the book as good as it can be. For their help and encouragement, I would like to thank the people at Microsoft Press – in particular, Karen Meredith, publicist; Barry Preppernau, senior technical reviewer; Salley Oberlin, editorial director; Joyce Cox, managing editor; and JoAnne Woodcock, senior editor. Special thanks also go to William Gladstone, my literary agent.

To the many other people who have contributed to this book: my appreciation for your efforts in making this an experience to be remembered. Thank you.

Bill Landreth
Poway, California
January 1985

Preface to the New Edition

When I wrote this book in 1985, many of you might have thought that issues of computer security belonged mostly in worlds like banking, industry, education, and government. After all, those institutions had the big, interesting computers. And those computers, open every day to people ranging from novices to systems experts, were vulnerable to unauthorized explorers. Besides, all those big, interesting, vulnerable computers could be accessed anonymously by telephone from around the corner or across the country. Your personal computer would almost surely be too small, too isolated, too...*personal*...to interest a hacker.

You would have been right. In 1985. But personal computers have changed in the last few years. They're bigger, more powerful, more widely used, more often connected via networks and telephone lines. Programs are passed around. So is information. So are pesky infections, some of which are silly, and some of which are destructive. These infections are called viruses, and in the past year or so some well-publicized viruses have focused attention on the problems of keeping all computers secure—small ones as well as big ones.

Recently, a number of viruses have infected personal computers: IBMs, Apple Macintoshes, and others. Some of these viruses were "benign"—more nuisance than nasty. Others, considerably more "virulent," were designed to destroy or damage information.

On a larger scale, computing-wise at any rate, in late 1988, a non-destructive but very prolific virus was released into a 60,000-computer network called ARPANET, which has existed since the 1960s. Although it was developed by the Advanced Research Projects Agency of the United States Department of Defense, ARPANET is not a top-secret information network. It's used by many research organizations and by universities such as the University of California at Berkeley and the Massachusetts Institute of Technology. ARPANET is a vehicle for ideas. It also became a carrier for a program that multiplied rapidly and spread to many computers—even to nonsecret parts of a second network called MILNET. According to *Time* magazine and other sources, this intruder was an impressive program that ran amok, spreading faster than even its inventor had expected. In the end, enormous amounts of time and energy were required to clean up infected computers, and uninfected computers had to be taken off the network to avoid contamination. With the clear vision that comes with hindsight, some experts now say that the incident was useful because it showed how important computer security is. Maybe they're right. But suppose the program hadn't been harmless. Suppose it had destroyed data. Would the lesson still have been worth the price?

AN UPDATE: VIRUSES

Capable of advancing from system to system, the virus program is captivating in concept, if rarely in execution. What is a virus? Do you need to worry about it? If so, why? Let's take a look.

Computer viruses are obviously named after the viruses that cause infections and diseases in living things. The name is appropriate because computer viruses have two characteristics in common with their DNA-based namesakes: They become active only in a suitable host, and they reproduce, sometimes wildly, when the environment is right.

Like the protein-based virus, the program virus therefore survives only by contact and duplication. To become active and reproduce, the program virus needs a host, a computer. In some cases, maybe the host computer must be an IBM personal computer; in others, maybe it must be an Apple Macintosh or a minicomputer running an operating system called UNIX.

A computer virus infects a computer's memory. It can reach the memory either by being read from an infected disk or by being transferred to the computer through a network connection or the telephone lines. Until it is in memory, the virus is inactive. You can, if you know how, find it and destroy it. Once in the computer's memory, however, the virus "wakes up" and becomes able to reproduce itself and to perform whatever mischief it might have been created to do—anything from displaying a message on your screen to altering information to destroying the data on a floppy or a hard disk. Once in memory and able to reproduce, the virus can, by gaining access to the computer's disk storage, save future generations by attaching copies of itself inconspicuously to valid information, including programs, data, even games. These new viruses can then be passed on to other computers, once again either on disk or by a network or a phone connection.

Viral attacks can even be made to capitalize on tools planted by another virus. As an entirely hypothetical example, let's say that a company named ProseWare is distributing WordWrite, a word processor. Somehow, a master copy of the program is "seeded" with a block of instructions that have nothing to do with word processing. Suppose, now, that these instructions are activated only on systems that are also running another program—let's say Networks' Netsoft.

Now everyone who uses an infected copy of WordWrite also gets a group of instructions that remain hidden and harmless until a particular virus finds and uses them. The virus that activates the instructions could be as small as 20 characters. No matter. The tiny virus discovers that it is on a machine running Networks' Netsoft and that it has access to the larger package of instructions in the infected WordWrite. The place is right, the time is right. The virus can trigger whatever parts of the larger package it was designed to, with whatever results the programmer intended.

Inside the Microcosm

Viruses aside for the moment, let's put things in perspective by taking a quick look at what happens inside your computer. Suppose that you want to remember, for old times' sake, that a particular client likes to go by his middle name, which is Bill. You tell a program to record this information. The entire procedure involves a trivial movement of numbers—from one location in your computer's memory to another. The final destination for Bill's name happens to be a holding area called a disk buffer, from which your computer takes information for storage on disk. Once the computer dedicates time to actually writing Bill's name on a disk, the whole procedure becomes merely another numbers game as the information gets marched from buffer to disk.

The important point is that all your computer (or at least the chip that is processing information) can ever do is carry out the next instruction in a list. This list moves from disk storage to memory, and it is fetched to the chip item by item. The next item on the list follows in succession, or it is pointed to by the current item. And it is here, more than anywhere else, that viral corruptions are seen—as data, if moved, or as program, if executed—as part of "the flow." Naturally, it is also very difficult to tell, from one instruction to the next, what is and what is not part of a virus.

How You Get Zapped

In order for any program to run on a computer, the first instruction must be loaded into the chip. This fact makes the computer's startup program one of the most likely targets for a virus infection. Why? Simply because a startup program is generally run every time you start or restart the computer. On almost any system, a simple restart can be enough to spread a virus from an infected machine to a disk that has not been write-protected. In other instances, transmission and activation could be traceable to various programs run from the native operating environment.

Everywhere to Hide

A virus can be designed to act in many different ways. On disk, the virus could exist as data—such as in a picture—within another (corrupted) program, or even in "empty" disk space. Once activated, the virus can take any of a number of courses, just as a disease-causing virus can. Among those courses are timed destruction, erasure or corruption of information, and, of course, infection of additional programs and disks.

On one hand, you might have a virus that only has fun. You might find that you occasionally lose a character you type or, perhaps, that your system will play a song on Christmas. On the other hand, after having a devious and destructive virus in your system for anywhere from a few minutes to several weeks or months, you could end up with a program that deletes incorrectly or one that copies erratically. Let's assume that the delete program not only erases information when you tell it to, but also marks the erased sections of the disk as unusable. Eventually, you'll find that your system is inexplicably "losing" hard-drive space. Each time you erase information, your hard drive becomes a little smaller. It's not getting smaller at all, of course. The virus is just manipulating the system so that all those erased areas appear to be "bad" and therefore unable to store information. A problem? Obviously. But what can you do about it?

When and how a virus obtains a chance to spread is very important to consider. Avoiding contact is, in fact, the only means of prevention although it's anywhere from difficult to impossible to do, especially if your computer is part of a network. The best advice to date is:

Keeping Clean

- *If you're setting up a system, or you use a floppy disk to start your system, be sure to use a "write-protected" floppy disk—that is, one that your computer cannot save any information on.*

- *Keep suspect disks away from your computer. These could be program disks other than ones that come directly from the manufacturer, disks on which you've copied programs from a source you cannot verify as "clean," or disks you've gotten from a friend of a friend of a friend....*

- *Don't move disks from machine to machine unless you know that they are not contaminated.*

- *If you run a network, or are part of one, consider one infection a sign that all machines, potentially, are infected.*

■ *If you are concerned about the possibility of contamination, find out about the anti-virus "vaccine" programs that are available to warn of possible infections. Even if a virus never appears on your system, at least you'll have one less worry.*

FROM THE
CROW'S NEST

How concerned should you be? No one can really answer that question. If you pass programs and information freely among a large group of people, you have more cause for concern than if you don't share disks and never connect to other computers. On the other hand, if cutting yourself off from the rest of your computing world would be a hardship, the risk of infection may be worth taking. It's your decision, really. Just be careful, as you are when the flu is "going around," and don't take foolish chances. Most importantly, if you discover an infection, find out where it came from and what was exposed. Treat this infection as you would any bodily infection: Prevent further spreading.

In the remainder of this book, you'll find out about the people who can't "just say no" to computers. Maybe it will give you some insights—not only about the lure of computers, but about computer security in general. We live in the "information age," and you might find those insights helpful...someday.

Bill Landreth
January 1989

■

OUT OF THE INNER CIRCLE

Prologue

It seems that the Age of Electronics has jumped out and caught a great many people more or less unprepared. Computer technology has evolved rapidly and in many directions in the past few years, and one of the offshoots of this development has been the rise of a new form of trespass: microcomputer hacking.

If you are a computer user, but not a computer professional, you may be wondering what goes on during those middle-of-the-night hackers' incursions that have been reported so often lately in the local and national press. If so, the following story may help give you a better feel for computers, hacking, and the interactions between hackers and computer professionals. The story is based on a real computer and a real corporation. Obviously, since I wasn't in the computer room, the dialogue is not real in the sense that I am quoting anyone. It *is* real, however, in the sense that it is based on many conversations I have had with dozens of people who are very much like the characters you will read about here.

BLINDMAN'S BUFF, HACKER STYLE

THE SCENE: *The control room in the computer center of one of the largest corporations in the world – an automobile manufacturer we'll call MegaCar International.* THE TIME: *12:30 a.m. – the beginning of the graveyard shift.*

Al, a system operator, has just arrived for work. He signs in with the armed guard at the security console located between the main entrance to the building and the hallway that leads to the computer center. Halfway down the hall, he shows his ID badge to another guard, then passes in front of twin television cameras at the entrance to the computer center. Before entering the control room, he goes through another, identical, set of security procedures.

There are good reasons for the tight security that surrounds Al's workstation: He controls access to the computers that hold information worth billions of dollars to MegaCar International – and to Mega-Car's competitors. Every night, the mainframes, minicomputers, and workstations of MegaCar's worldwide computer network process scores of secret details on next year's automobile designs, along with dozens of high-level, strategic electronic memos and thousands of scraps of financial and technical information.

This control center is the "brain" of the worldwide network, where everything comes together. It is also where the most intense action takes place when things go wrong. Common problems are handled by specialized troubleshooting computers, or by system operators at local and regional computer centers around the world. But if the troubleshooting computers break down, or the local system operators can't pinpoint the problem, or the network itself runs into trouble, then Al and his colleagues must figure out what to do to keep the numbers crunching and the data flowing.

Despite his title, Al is no typical "system operator." His actual duties would probably suggest the title of *security officer* or *on-call handyman.* In addition to keeping the printers full of paper, keeping track of the reels of magnetic tape, and helping users out with minor problems (as all system operators must do), Al is one of several highly trained support people who are on call twenty-four hours a day to resolve any potential hangups or security breaches in and among the many "nodes" of MegaCar's electronic "filing cabinets."

But whether or not your job includes watching for intruders, being a system operator on the graveyard shift means going through long periods of inactivity punctuated by brief periods of frenzied work. Al isn't anticipating anything different tonight. Seated in front of a bank of computer terminals, a cup of coffee in one hand and a printout of the evening's computer activities in the other, he prepares for another uneventful round of crossword puzzles and solitaire, with perhaps some troubleshooting thrown in. Like some system operators, though, since he really likes computers and thinks of them as both a hobby and a profession, tonight he is planning a special diversion: COBOL, instead of cards.

But on this particular night the routine is broken by some puzzling activity on a VAX superminicomputer at the corporation's top-secret research center.

George, Al's colleague at the neighboring station, is browsing through the usage logs that record the activity of all the computers in MegaCar's far-flung network. As he does, he happens to notice that the VAX is working hard—very hard. Even though the log shows only one person using the computer, the workload on the machine's central processor is high enough for ten or more users.

It all starts with a few quiet words.

"Al, I think something weird is happening on the net."

"Which node?" Al replies, putting down his COBOL text and mentally preparing for a debugging job that might take thirty seconds, and then again might take all night, to clean up the problem.

"4316. That's one of the R&D hosts in New York."

"The New York VAX? What's wrong?"

"I don't know. Why don't you echo terminal 23 and see what you can make of it?"

"Right."

Al pulls his chair closer to his computer console, puts both hands on the keyboard, and rapidly taps out a string of commands. Then he sits back and watches the central display monitor, as row after row of glowing green letters and numbers march across the screen. The central monitor is showing him everything that is happening on the VAX computer halfway across the country, in New York.

After a few seconds, Al reaches for a telephone.

"George, get me the name and home phone number of account STD123." Al's voice betrays his concern. His simple check of the activity on the VAX has made it obvious that something is wrong. The exact nature of the problem is not clear, but Al is certain that this is no run-of-the-mill software glitch. Either someone has been authorized to use excessive amounts of computer time every hour without letting the system operators know – or someone is doing something they shouldn't be doing with that computer.

As soon as the account holder's name and phone number appear on his screen, Al makes the call. "Hello, Dr. Saunders? This is Al Frankston, the head system operator at the computer center. Sorry to disturb you at this hour, but we're reading some strange activity on the VAX. Are you using your account on that computer right now?"

Like many other high-level personnel at the research center, Dr. Saunders has a computer terminal at home, so he can use the central computer via telephone link if he wants to have access to the day's research results or continue his own research. Al and George look at each other, as if to say, "Are you thinking what I'm thinking?" George listens to Al's phone conversation with interest as he continues to study the computer display still echoing the VAX's puzzling activity.

"Thank you," Al replies, as Dr. Saunders confirms that he is, indeed, using the VAX. "Oh, one more thing," he adds. "Would you tell me your social security number? . . . No, it isn't anything significant. It's just a little mix-up with our user account numbers. We'll have it straightened out by morning. Good night."

Although he can see the same thing Al sees by looking at the display screen of his own console, George wheels his chair over to Al's station and watches with raised eyebrows as Al verifies the social security number he's been given.

"It checks out," Al says, sounding puzzled.

"You mean Dr. Saunders really is logged on now?" George asks, almost disappointed. "I was half hoping the account was being used by that hacker we almost caught last week."

Al looks back at his screen. "No, I guess not. . . . But there has to be a reason for that phantom time," he mumbles, scratching his chin.

4

A loud voice suddenly breaks the quiet in the control room. "Hey Al!" a technician half shouts from the other side of the room. "There's a message for you coming over the laser printer. I think you better come and take a look at it."

Al and George exchange a quick glance, knowing looks creeping onto their faces. They leave their workstations and walk to a printer about the size of a washing machine. Pieces of paper are quietly dropping into a large bin at the rate of about one sheet per second. George grabs one of the pages.

There is a large headline at the top: "A note to the chief system operator on duty." Below that, in slightly smaller type, are the words "Please make sure the sysop reads this. Thank you." In normal type, the message continues: "It should be noted that computer print-outs currently are not legal evidence in court."

George starts to read the message aloud, his voice a mixture of annoyance, admiration, and puzzlement. "It is our opinion that you should be more careful about your design plans for the TRX project." His voice drops and grows more serious as he reads the next sentence. "One of us suggested that maybe we should sell the information to another car company."

Now, Al starts reading over George's shoulder – and they both read silently. "Several of us don't think there is anything wrong with ripping off a company as big as yours. But some of us think that industrial espionage would break our unwritten hacker laws. We may vote on the subject in the near future. In any case, we would like to have one or more unlimited user accounts so that we do not have to go to the trouble of calling your ALF node by way of SYSNET12. We can't use 1200 baud through SYSNET12. Of course, if you decide to grant us a little assistance of this sort, it could be that we would all be more kindly disposed toward your institution when we vote on what to do with the TRX data."

"What do you think?" asks George.

Al is leafing through the now very large pile of paper in the output bin. "They're all the same. What's TRX?"

George thinks momentarily. "I don't know. They must have made it up. It has to be a bluff."

Seconds later, as if on cue, another printer starts shooting out more sheets of paper. Al looks grim when he sees what these latest mystery sheets have to say. "Well, maybe they're bluffing about selling the stuff, but I don't think they're bluffing about having it. These look suspiciously like design memos for next year's car!"

Al studies the new sheets for a minute, then continues, tension rising in his voice. "We still don't know *where* those hackers are! All we know is, they're *not* using Dr. Saunders' account."

Suddenly, a new thought dawns on them, and they almost run in their hurry to get back to their workstations. Both sysops look at their screens. "They may have altered the monitor program on my terminal so I can't find them or their account," Al mutters, sounding hopeful. "But if they did, they may not have changed the programs that run on our other terminals. I'm going to break out of my version and use some of the other monitoring programs – see if there is anything different between mine and the others' log-on sequences or lists of account names."

After several minutes of frantic typing, George walks over to Al's station. He looks at the screen, pondering something, then he walks back to his own station, glances at his own screen, and bursts out in surprise, "Someone new is logging onto the VAX. Turn your monitor program back on."

Al stops his checking and runs his monitoring program. "That 'someone' is using an old test account. I could have sworn we killed them all months ago," he says.

George is watching the same display. "Funny, but I thought so, too. Either we let that one slip, or those hackers reactivated it. But it doesn't make any difference. No one's authorized to use that account now, anyway, so. . . ."

"Right. So we have our hacker!" Al sounds proud of himself. He has been worried, but now the game is over. "Let's break in and let him know how we feel before we throw him off the system."

"Oh, yeah," says George sarcastically. "And while you're at it, ask him how he got that valuable data." George holds up one finger, as if counting. "And then see what he plans on doing with it." He holds up a second finger. "And find out how. . ."

Al interrupts: "Okay, okay. So we still have a lot of work to do. Let's get started."

They both go over to a single terminal and Al starts to type. He uses the monitoring program to trace the source of the intrusion, then gives the system a few commands that allow him to break in and communicate with the person using the unauthorized account. Then, he types: "OK. We know who you are and what you did. Either cooperate or we will press full charges."

After a short pause, a rapidly typed reply appears on the display screen: "Yeah, sure. I guess you guys are just too smart for me. Anyway, all humor aside, I was just sent to this account by my friends to get your reply to our offer. Have you decided to give us those unlimited accounts yet?"

Al chuckles while he types. "Why should we? We can just have you arrested! Besides, it isn't our computer. We can't just decide to assign an unlimited account to somebody outside the corporation."

The hacker types back: "Oh, so you'll just call up the police and say, 'There's this hacker on our system and we suspect he just may be somewhere in the 50 states. We can't be sure exactly where...?' It's never worked before, but what the hell—go ahead and try. It'll be fun. Meanwhile we'll play with this TRX stuff."

George now pushes in front of Al and commandeers the keyboard, typing: "We have you traced. We know who you are and where you are. We just want to ask you a few questions."

"About security, right?" the hacker types back. "Well, I'm sure you will have no more security problems if you help us out. You have fairly good security without our advice. Only the best could have done what we've done. And that's who we are: the best. So I guess you could say that your future security problems are pretty much up to us. There is another possibility, though."

George, still at the keyboard, hesitates a moment, then types back: "And what's that?"

"Well, we could post our information about your system on a few bulletin boards. Then a few hundred lesser talents would try to log on. I'll bet a crasher would have fun with this VAX or that beautiful DEC-20 in Detroit. And there's always the possibility that another large car company would let us use their system in exchange for the data we have. You can never tell about these things."

Al is not amused. He snaps a pencil in half while thinking over a reply. George is almost speechless. "Arrogant little..." he is beginning to say, when Al finally types: "We'll have to think about this. You guys might just be half as smart as you think you are. By the way, how do we reach you? Can you give us your phone number?"

"I'm glad the bad news hasn't ruined your sense of humor," replies their distant adversary. "Let's just say that we'll get in touch in our own way, in our own time. The way we always do. In the meantime, I guess it wouldn't hurt to give you a little tidbit for your trouble. Why don't you tell all your users that SECRET is a lousy choice for a secret password? I'll bet I've cracked a dozen systems with that one. Stay tuned. And keep designing those sexy cars. Bye."

Although, in actuality, hackers and most system operators tend to speak a much less comprehensible language, and most hacking experiences tend to involve much less conspicuous companies, hackers did manage to find and look at secret design specifications and test results. These particular hackers did not attempt, or ever intend, to sell or trade "MegaCar's" priceless files to a competitor ... but someone else might not have been so "honorable." That's the point of this book, and if you are concerned about computer security, whether as a computer professional or as an interested citizen, I hope you will benefit from what I learned as The Cracker, inside the Inner Circle.

CHAPTER ONE

Inside the Inner Circle

There's been a lot of publicity about long-distance tapping into the programs and information files of large computer systems. So much, in fact, that many people who meet me for the first time are somewhat surprised and say something along the lines of, "You're not what I expected."

Movies, television, and news articles have characterized hackers as everything from technological delinquents to playful whiz kids who can start the countdown to World War III – even before they have learned to swim. Where's the truth? Probably somewhere in between. So perhaps the best way to introduce you to hackers and hacking is by presenting my "credentials."

My name is Bill Landreth. I am nineteen years old, and I live in southern California. About a dozen members of the FBI and quite a few members of the hacking community, however, know me better as The Cracker, one of the leaders of an "invitation-only" group of hackers called the Inner Circle. I began hacking when I was fourteen, but my career came to a rather abrupt end in 1983, when I was caught and indicted for computer fraud—tapping into the GTE Telemail computer network based in Vienna, Virginia. Since then, I have been convicted of the charge and am now serving three years' probation.

If you are wondering what I am like, I can tell you the same things I told the judge in federal court: Although it may not seem like it, I am pretty much a normal American teenager. I don't drink, smoke, or take drugs. I don't steal, assault people, or vandalize property. The only way in which I am really different from most people is in my fascination with the ways and means of learning about computers that don't belong to me.

GETTING
STARTED

It was mid-1979 when I got hooked on computers. I was fourteen, and I had just brought my first computer home from Radio Shack. It was a TRS-80 Model I, Level II, with a whole 16K of memory and a cassette tape drive for "mass storage." With tax, the entire system came to just under $1000, half of which came from my savings, and the other half from my parents. I spent all my after-school hours learning how to operate this computer, and soon found that no matter how much I thought I knew, there was always more to be learned.

Like many computer enthusiasts and almost all hackers, I taught myself how to program – from reading books and looking at other people's programs, and by asking questions of friends. For the first six months, I kept busy learning BASIC. There was always a new command to learn that would make programming a bit easier, and as I became more familiar with BASIC, there were all sorts of tricks I could figure out to make my programs run better or faster, or to do things I had thought were impossible. After becoming comfortable with BASIC, I started all over again with a new language and, soon after that, I started to teach myself Z-80 assembly language, which is a humanized version of the computer's own internal machine code.

This kind of learning was a welcome change from schoolwork. Programming was never boring, and there seemed to be no end to what I could learn about it. Best of all, I could study what I wanted, whenever and however I wanted to. No matter what language I was using or what specific goal I had in mind, it seemed that there would always be something interesting left to learn.

With computers (as with most other subjects, I suppose) one thing leads naturally to another, and while I was becoming fluent in assembly language, I found that I was also learning more and more about the machine itself. I still wanted to know about all the various computer languages, but now I also wanted to know about the inner workings of *all* computers.

One of the aspects of the TRS-80 that fascinated me most was the intricacy of its operating system, the set of programs that told the computer how to run itself – how to "understand" what I typed, how to display information, how to keep all its parts working in harmony. Like most operating systems, the TRS-80's included a small number of very basic commands that any user had to know in order to operate the machine successfully, and a larger number of more complex commands that only avid programmers would care about.

I was no longer interested in simply *using* the machine. I wanted to find out for myself what made it tick, and the operating system offered a wealth of information. The farther I went, the more I learned about the way these programs were structured and the way they controlled the operation of the computer. Eventually, my interest in the insides of my TRS-80 took me to bigger and better things: mainframe and minicomputer operating systems, which are orders of magnitude more complicated (and hence more fascinating) than a personal computer's operating system. But the TRS-80's operating system is still where it all began.

*The
Magic Door*

Just about the time I was beginning to feel I understood my TRS-80, I got an Apple II. I had owned the TRS-80 for about a year when my parents, who recognized my mania for computers, bought the Apple for me. The learning and exploring started over again, but this time it moved more quickly, because I now had a foundation to build on.

Everything I'd learned and done up to this point, of course, was perfectly legal and no more – or less – involved than any other enthusiastic hobbyist's efforts would be. Then, I found out about the truly big and powerful computers called mainframes, minicomputers, and superminis. The kind that are often used from a remote location, via an ordinary telephone line.

It all started soon after I got my Apple, when I acquired a dumb terminal. If computer terminology is new to you, a dumb terminal is a "brainless" keyboard-and-screen device; it does not have any computing power of its own, but it does allow you to hook up to other computers, which can be around the corner or around the world, wherever a cable or a communications link can connect the two machines. I didn't acquire a dumb terminal because I wanted to break into big computers. In fact, the situation was exactly the reverse: A friend loaned me the terminal, and in the process of finding out what to do with it, I discovered the world of minis and mainframes.

Since this borrowed terminal had a built-in communications device called a modem, I discovered that I could connect the terminal to other computers over my home phone line. At first, I used the terminal to call up the numbers of some bulletin boards I knew of. As the name implies, bulletin boards are message-mediating computers that act as a kind of information center for the computer community. Anyone who knows how to do it can set up a computer as a bulletin board; many computer clubs and other special-interest groups use them extensively. In fact, private bulletin boards later became an important way for Inner Circle members to exchange information, and one in particular – illegally set up on the GTE Telemail network – led to the retirement of The Cracker.

When I was a newcomer to telecommunications, however, there were only a few public, non-hacker bulletin boards for me to choose from – one was local, and there were another five to seven within my area code. I found out about them through various hobbyist magazines, but no one ever seemed to use these things.

Then, a friend told me he knew the phone number to a large corporate computer. He had no use for the number, so he gave it to me, and I called it.

By all rights, that first attempt should have been my last. Sure, I had called the number and the computer had answered, but now what? A large, multi-user computer doesn't sit there and chat just because you feel like calling. It has to keep track of who's doing what, and when, and it does so by "crediting" every task, no matter how large or how small, to someone's account – an account that can only be used by giving the computer an account-name/secret-password combination it recognizes as valid. No account, no access; as far as the computer is concerned, you don't exist.

After calling and seeing the computer's prompt for an account name, I started to try first names. For some unknown reason, I stuck to three-character names and tried the same ones as both the account name and the password. First, I tried DAN. No luck. Next, I tried JIM. Nope, too bad. My third try was LEE. Against odds no gambler would ever bet on, it worked. My luck was incredible: Three tries, with no clues, and I hit on a valid account/password combination.

It's hard to describe all the excitement I felt when LEE unlocked the magic door to that corporate computer. I was expecting to see ACCESS DENIED for the third time; instead the screen cleared and the name of the company that owned the account appeared on the screen. I guess a winner of the Irish Sweepstakes must feel the same way I did then; I really thought I had no chance of getting into that computer. To my surprise and delight, my first attempt at hacking on an unknown computer was a success! I had opened the door to a whole new kind of computer to learn about. But what was on the other side of that door? And how was I going to find my way around once I got in?

Learning The Ropes

Soon after getting onto that first system, I discovered that I didn't need a users' manual for guidance. All I had to do was type HELP, and the system would teach me how to use it. It wasn't a complete blabbermouth, since it did refuse to tell how to get more accounts. But before I was discovered by the system operator about three months later, I had learned enough about the operating system to have discovered about thirty accounts. It was here that I learned just how complex a computer can be and came to respect the amount of time and effort that had gone into making the operating system work. Hundreds of people may have worked hundreds of hours each to make this system what it was, with each person contributing a little bit to the whole. The system was so big, so complex, that not even *they* could know every possible detail about it.

While I was exploring that first computer, I was also using the dumb terminal to look around for interesting microcomputer bulletin-board systems. Eventually, I ran across a few bulletin boards that were used by "software pirates"– people who trade illegally copied computer software with one another. On these boards, I would run across a bit of information on "hacking" every now and then.

I wanted to get more involved with larger computer systems, so I established computer contact, through these bulletin boards, with those few people who called themselves hackers. And through these contacts, I soon found that there were many more of these bulletin-board systems around the country. Each one of them offered more information for me to try out – new phone numbers, account names, passwords, special tips, and so on.

As I used and tested all this new information, I expanded my knowledge of different operating systems running on different mainframe computers. Up until then, I had learned how to use the "help" feature to learn the basic operating commands, and I had learned to look for "test" accounts that had been set up (and never deleted or deactivated) when the system was installed. But when I started communicating with other hackers, I learned what types of commands are likely to be on *any* operating system, and I learned how to find them. I became familiar with the ins and outs of the most common operating systems, and I found out about some of the security weaknesses of the most common systems. I also learned, through trial and error as much as anything else, how to go about trying to acquire more powerful accounts on a particular system. An account with a programmer's privileges, for example, would, by its nature, allow me to control the system more than, say, a data-entry clerk's account. Once I started putting this knowledge to work, I could start trading information with other hackers.

The Hacker's
Currency

Information is the currency of the hacker's bulletin-board culture, and trading is the means of exchange. Accounts take a lot of work to get, so most hackers are unlikely to post information publicly, when they can trade it for more information from other hackers. In addition, an average hacker only acquires four or five new accounts in a year, and all

14

but maybe one of these accounts die within six or seven months. That same hacker could, however, trade those four or five accounts four or five times each, and those exchanges would net him as many as twenty-five different accounts for the year.

A more important reason for trading, though, is to keep account information out of the hands of novices. Often, when novices get hold of publicly posted information, they abuse it by sending obscenities to the system operator, destroying information, changing passwords, or removing accounts. Moral arguments aside, hackers dislike this kind of abuse, because accounts that are abused die quickly.

Obviously, I wasn't born a high-level hacker. Like many newcomers who later turned to me for advice, I sought information from those more experienced than I. For example, one very good hacker who called himself Bootleg showed me the power of large networks. Basic information like this is very important to a hacker. It also isn't much good without the skills that can only be developed through practice. And either a high degree of skill or a sense of hacker ethics (more on this shortly), is needed to keep this information from becoming dangerous to computer systems and the information they contain. Both my own feelings and the things I learned from hackers like Bootleg taught me these lessons – and served to whet my appetite for more knowledge, the kind I could discover on my own.

Becoming The Cracker

When I first became involved with hacking, I learned that I was not expected to leave my real name anywhere. In fact, it was considered fairly stupid to do so. Everyone involved with hacking chose a "handle," like Bootleg, that was used as a name on all the hacker bulletin boards. I chose to become The Cracker, and set out to establish a reputation among other hackers.

I could have decided to stay low-key, but I was eager to gain more information than I already had, so I posted messages on hacker bulletin boards, advertising that I was willing to trade any information I had for any information anyone else had. I was a novice in this newfound "brotherhood," but I realized that I could be accepted as a bona fide hacker relatively quickly by trading only the highest quality information. (In most cases, "trade information" means "I'll give you what you need now, and next time you get something good, let me know.") Within a few months of my first postings, the word started to get around: The Cracker is OK.

I learned as much as I could as fast as I could, and after several months of intensive hacking and information-trading, The Cracker was no longer a novice. I knew a lot about hacking by then, and because I liked to share what I knew, I gained the reputation of being someone to go to if you were having trouble. Others hackers began to request advice, and I continued to improve the quality of my information and knowledge by exploring as many computers as I could find. In many cases, another hacker would ask me to try an account to see if I could figure out what system it was on and who owned it. I got a lot of exposure to different machines that way.

After a while, people would leave messages saying, "I know you can't help me, but I would like to get onto this system. . . ." To their surprise, I could usually help out. They needed someone who knew more about a particular operating system than they did – someone who had perhaps seen the inside before – or who might have a few new ideas about how to guess passwords. As The Cracker's reputation grew, answering such requests became a matter of pride. No matter how difficult the question happened to be, I would sit at the terminal for five, ten, twenty hours at a time, until I had the answer.

FORMATION OF THE INNER CIRCLE

When I first started hacking, it took a while to find other hackers. Hacker bulletin-board systems were few and far between. But a year later, things started changing rapidly. The microcomputer revolution was putting thousands of machines into thousands of homes every week, so the number of people who began to explore telecommunications and large computers increased dramatically in 1981 and 1982. New hackers popped into the networks every day.

During this time, it became very difficult to tell who it was safe to trade information with. Sometimes, the person you gave the information to would abuse the account himself, thus rendering it useless to you. Other times, the person you gave the information to would post it publicly and claim that it was he who took the time and effort to get the account – still rendering the account useless to you, but also using your hours of work to better his reputation. In any case, if you gave information to the wrong person, you probably would not get anything in return.

It was during this time that the Inner Circle was formed, and the person most responsible for its formation was the person who taught me the most about hacking. His handle was Alpha Hacker. I "met" him through one of the bulletin boards, and it was clear from our first communications that he was a hacker among hackers. We have never met face to face, and I still don't know his real name, but he introduced me to several key hacking techniques. Alpha knew tricks that I had never dreamed of.

When I was a beginner, Alpha Hacker had been one of those who appreciated the quality of my information. He had been able to gain access to a number of powerful accounts as a result of what he learned from me, and we began to exchange messages. It became obvious to both of us that we were two of a kind and, like any specialists, we enjoyed the opportunity to learn from each other as much as we enjoyed solving problems for other hackers.

Alpha Hacker told me he was interested in forming a kind of high-level hackers' guild, because of his concern over who might get their hands on the most useful and sensitive pieces of information we turned up. The concept of the Inner Circle was that the best hackers would meet on private bulletin boards and post their information for other members to see. We would create password-based security systems on these special bulletin boards – security systems strong enough to resist the efforts of other hackers. With these systems in place, we would not have to worry about trading information; all we had to do was place information in the message base and check back every now and then to see what was there.

The Inner Circle was formed in early 1982, when Alpha Hacker called me with the idea (he was one of the few hackers to whom I had given my phone number). I agreed to join, and we started to pick out the hackers we both wanted to invite into the group. We picked the best hackers that we knew – those who seemed to fit in with our concept. And to make sure we kept strict control over membership and over the way information was used, we decided to form a kind of tribunal that we called the Inner Circle Seven.

Our organization and our membership policy actually turned out to be a very timely idea (from our point of view, anyway), because not long after we formed the Inner Circle the movie *WarGames* was released, and in its wake came a flood of eager-beaver new hackers. In a matter of months the number of self-proclaimed hackers tripled, then quadrupled. You couldn't get through to any of the old bulletin boards any more – the telephone numbers were busy all night long. Even worse, you could delicately work to gain entrance to a system, only to find dozens of novices blithely tromping around the files.

Membership Requirements

When Alpha Hacker and I were deciding whom to invite into the Inner Circle and whom not to include, we kept two different requirements in mind. First, we wanted to make sure the members were good hackers. Each member had to have proven he could get good information on his own. That way, we would be assured that each member could, and would, contribute to keeping the Inner Circle's information base at a fairly high level. Second, we agreed that every hacker in the group must be the kind of person who could be trusted not to abuse account information given to him by other hackers.

The fact that we tried to invite only those people who already met these two requirements quickly resulted in an unwritten "code of ethics" that was, and remained, the philosophy that held the Inner Circle together. This code had two practical uses for our group. The most apparent was that information we gathered would remain useful for a longer period of time. But just as importantly, our approach served to keep the system operators on our side. If the code had ever been written, it would have looked something like this:

- *No Inner Circle member will ever delete or damage information that belongs to a legitimate user of the system in any way that the member cannot easily correct himself.*

- *No member will leave another hacker's name or phone number on any computer system. He will leave his own on a system only at his own risk.*

▬ *All members are expected to obtain and contribute their own account information, rather than use only information given to them by other members.*

We had many good reasons to follow these basic rules. But the most important, as far as the Inner Circle was concerned, had to do with the basic principle of respecting other people's property and information. We were explorers, not spies, and to us, damaging computer files was not only clumsy and inelegant – it was wrong.

In fact, we had one occasion to test our beliefs a few months after the Inner Circle was formed. One of our members, who went by the handle Mandrake, had deleted some information and, in general, had caused trouble on a computer system. When asked if and why he did it, Mandrake said yes he did – because he was bored. Very soon after we heard about the incident, we closed the Inner Circle to him. Of course, that meant changing the password procedures on all of our secret bulletin boards. We didn't want to go to that much trouble very often, so we screened new applicants more carefully after that, and even at the height of our activities, in mid-1983, the Inner Circle numbered no more than fifteen.

INNER CIRCLE CAPERS

The Inner Circle was a strong group, and we found there was a definite advantage to making it easy for the best hackers to interact with one another. But I'd like to emphasize that the Inner Circle was interested in *computers* – not in the organizations that owned and used them. At least 95 percent of the institutions whose computers the Inner Circle penetrated would not interest anyone.

On the other hand, you are no doubt curious about what we saw, and this is probably as good a time as any to satisfy that curiosity. To protect the privacy of the institutions involved, I will not mention their names or give you any specific details that I think might compromise their computer systems.

Bank

At one point, an Inner Circle member discovered a demonstration computer that was owned by a very large banking firm. The account name and password were obvious: BANK. In itself, this account was not worth very much. It showed you a menu of options that looked quite powerful, but the menu was only a simulation, intended to give first-time users a flavor of how the system worked. This demonstration system was not useless, though, because I was able to break out of the simulation program and get into the actual operating system.

The system itself didn't have anything that was new to me, so I was quickly bored with it, even though I saw messages that were the actual substance of multimillion-dollar transactions. Someone naive or someone whose passion was for money, rather than knowledge, could have found the sight very... intriguing, even though, in most cases, a hacker would have little, if any, hope of transferring funds. On the other hand, I do know of a case in which someone stumbled, purely by accident, right into the fund-transfer system of a different computer. Hmm....

Newspaper

At one time during the height of the Inner Circle's activities, one of our members found a computer on a large network that did not seem to do very much. Whenever we called it, the computer would send ! as a prompt to our terminals, but we could get it to do nothing more. Not very exciting.

Of course, right away we tried all sorts of things. We tried HELP and INFO, which are built into many computers to keep users from getting lost. We tried the old standards, such as LOGIN and HELLO. When words failed, we tried various control-character combinations; Control-E, for instance, sometimes causes a computer to identify itself. None of these obvious tactics worked.

One day, I was trying a few things that we may have missed, and discovered that when I typed in the letters O P E N, the ! prompt was replaced with #.

I tried O P E N a second time. It worked again, and this time the distant computer replied READY TO TAKE INPUT. I had to assume the computer was waiting for a message of some kind, and I knew that if I was supposed to enter a message, I would also need some way of telling the computer when I was through. I hit the return key; when that didn't work, I started pushing various characters

20

to try and tell the computer I didn't want to input anything. I very soon found that hitting Control-X got the reply INPUT ACCEPTED, and a few seconds later, I saw:

1 - SEND STORY TO WORD PROCESSING
2 - SEND STORY TO EDITOR
3 - SEND STORY TO WIRE
4 - ABORT STORY

I tried hitting the return key at this point, and received a message telling me to call a certain phone number for help, if needed. I decided instead to abort my nonexistent story, hoping that the owners of the computer would not notice my incursion and, perhaps, increase security. Right after I made my choice, the computer hung up on me.

I did call the phone number I'd been given, and reached a large newspaper based on the East Coast. When I told the Inner Circle what I had learned, we realized that, if we discovered the correct format for submitting stories, we might have stories of our own printed. Though it would be all but impossible to print a major falsehood — because of the checks that exist within the newspaper — printing fairly normal, well-written stories containing subtle messages or jokes should not be a major problem. Knowing was better than doing to the Inner Circle, though, so we never used this service.

School

During one of our travels, this time to a computer in Texas, we ran across a group of high-school students who were using various accounts to do their computer-programming classwork assignments. They were using BASIC to write programs to do simple things, such as figure the amount of interest paid on a loan, or find the prime numbers between 1 and 10,000.

The computer itself held little interest for us, but because we thought that a few of the high-school users could be hackers on the side, we started to look around the system. These students were not very advanced in the computer field, so it wasn't too long before we found a few programs that had been written incorrectly. We decided to help out a little bit. Each of us chose one student and rewrote the program the student had undertaken. We did it using programming techniques that were far beyond the BASIC they were using, and to avoid confusing anyone, we were careful to document our own versions well, so that both the students and the teachers could learn from the experience.

Phone Company

Sometimes, it is not the computer that interests a hacker the most, or the name of the company, or even the information on the computer. While rare, it sometimes happens that the procedure of the company interests us more than anything else. It would greatly interest us all, for example, to learn exactly how the FBI went about keeping track of us, or to learn what plans NASA has to make sure its funding is continued. In this caper, the Inner Circle learned a little about how phone companies operate.

I should note that the term telephone company can mean one of many different companies. Since the breakup of the Bell system, not only are there different telephone companies in different locations, there can also be a choice of different phone companies in a single location. In some places, a telephone company's computers can actually be accessed by outside callers. Because of a few fairly recent high-publicity cases, however, phone-system computers have become quite secure in most respects.

Phone companies attain this level of security by having more than one system. Different systems are used for different things and, in most cases, only one of them is always available for outside access.

Generally, one computer system is required to be available to other branches or to other phone companies to simplify billing. This system is "secure," because information cannot be changed – it can only be seen. I have limited experience, and only with this particular system, but I assume that all phone-company computers are somewhat similar: A person from one branch of the phone company calls the computer that is local to the customer in question. The caller then enters a password (usually only a password, as far as I can tell) and the customer's phone number. The result is a page or more of customer billing information in a format similar to your monthly phone bill. A hacker's uses for this information would obviously be limited – say, to find out who owns phone number 555-9483, or to see how many times an employee is calling someone at a rival company every month. For the most part, it was just interesting to know something that most people didn't know about the phone company.

The problem with a credit bureau is that it must be accessed by a large *Credit* number of people. The twenty-year-old salesman selling a stove to a couple has just as much right to check on a person's credit as the company selling a $500,000 yacht to a millionaire.

In many cases the person needing the information never uses the computer directly, but he still needs the information. This need for accessibility makes the computers that hold credit records – yours, mine, and everyone else's – fairly non-secure because, even with the most expensive and careful procedures, there are still those people who need the information and must have access. And, as you'll see later in this book, people are the weakest link in the security chain. I doubt that five minutes ever passed when members of the Inner Circle didn't have all the information they needed to get credit information on anyone they would have liked to check on . . . and we certainly weren't the first. Police have reported that prostitutes and drug dealers have sometimes been known to have access to credit information, too.

This kind of information is potentially much more damaging than you might first think. For starters, access to it is a pure and simple invasion of privacy. Second, unscrupulous people could use other people's credit and names for about any purpose the rightful owners might – including credit cards, social security, or credit rating for the purpose of getting a loan.

CHAPTER TWO

A Look at the Past

T he term *hacker* goes back about twenty years, to the days of antiseptic computer rooms and stacked boxes of punched cards that you were told not to "spindle, fold, or mutilate." In those days, like now, a hacker was someone who simply wanted to eat, breathe, and sleep computers.

As computer technology has evolved, however, the definition of a hacker has taken on different shades of meaning, too. In the late 1960s to the mid-1970s, the term *hacker* was applied to anyone doing anything with computers, but especially to someone who worked on programming the machines. Then, from the mid- to late-1970s, a hacker was someone with enough of a love of computers to build his own from the limited resources of the time. Later still, between 1979 and 1981, a hacker was most likely someone so fascinated by computers that his involvement with them approached or passed the point of "working too much" – this was the "classic" hacker who ran around with a calculator in one pocket and pieces of computer in the other.

Then, starting about 1981 or 1982, the personal-computer market burst open. Software and hardware were designed to allow freer communication than ever before between large and small computers. This brought about the most recent change in the definition of a hacker: A person who often attempts to gain unauthorized access to large systems by using his personal computer equipment.

The recent publicity about the movie *WarGames* and the arrests of teenage hackers, such as the Wisconsin group that called themselves the 414s, has brought the term to the attention of the public for the first time. As a result, I think the latest definition is probably here to stay. This chapter, though, is mostly about earlier "breeds" of hackers who, whether they ever dreamt it or not, had an effect on the hackers of today.

THE SIXTIES
HACKER

Back in the early 1960s, in the primitive days of hacker history long before ordinary teenagers could afford to install personal computers in their bedrooms, a group of young people about the same age as today's hackers began to create a new culture. These were young computer wizards, many of them school dropouts, and they were employed by the artificial-intelligence and computer-systems research laboratories at the Massachusetts Institute of Technology (MIT). They worked on a project known as "MAC" – a fabulous venture whose initials have been (and apparently were intended to be) interpreted as standing for Multiple-Access Computers, Machine-Aided Cognition or, at MIT itself, Man Against Computers.

Legends say some of these first hackers were a rather motley, wild, and eccentric crew, but there was a good reason why the MIT administration permitted them to work in this ultra-sophisticated department (which, though few of them knew of it, was funded by ARPA, the Advanced Research Projects Agency of the Defense Department): The MIT laboratories didn't just *use* state-of-the-art hardware – they *created* it. These young programmers knew the system better than anyone else, so they were more qualified than anyone else to create the software that would bring the state-of-the-art hardware of those days to life.

Although they were often untidy, kept strange hours, and spoke a language that only other hackers could understand, the MAC hackers weren't just fringe fanatics. They were the most progressive software designers around, at a time when a whole new kind of computer was evolving – a computer that would pave the way for the personal computers of today.

The MAC hackers wrote the first chess-playing programs, and they also worked with a computer scientist named John McCarthy to develop a high-level programming language called LISP for artificial-intelligence programmers to use. In addition, they were the first to put together the sophisticated programs that are known today as "expert systems." But perhaps the hackers' greatest accomplishment came from the role they played in the creation of computer time-sharing. A time-shared computer system is one in which several people can use the computer at the same time, and time-sharing was a turning point in computer evolution because it made computers more accessible to programmers.

Up until the MAC hackers and other groups of programmers created time-sharing systems, programmers had no way to interact directly with the computer. Big mainframe computers and punched cards were state of the art. Programmers had to submit their decks of punched cards to system operators – the high priests of the mainframe world – and wait for the results. And the results, good or bad, came back as a paper printout. If the program needed only one correction, the entire stack of punched cards had to be submitted again and again.

All this was going on in 1959 and 1960, and it seemed as though mainframes and teletype machines were doing their best to keep computers and programmers apart.

Then, the MAC hackers and their colleagues began to create a special kind of operating system, a set of programs that would enable a computer to interact directly with several programmers at the same time, and to display results immediately on TV-like screens (cathode-ray tubes) rather than on teletype printouts.

Because they created the time-sharing framework that allowed everyone else to use the new computer system, the MAC hackers (now called system programmers) had a certain power over the other users, including their bosses and teachers. One aspect of this power was an ability to "crash the system" by running a particular program. A system crash would usually dump all unsaved data into computer oblivion, and would lock up the system until the hacker or someone else came up with a way to fix it.

In the early days of time-sharing, crashing – testing the system's limits – was encouraged in the MAC project, because programs that crashed the system did so by exploiting a bug, a flaw in the system software. Everyone wanted to find and fix all the system's bugs and vulnerabilities, so this kind of deliberate horseplay was a vital part of the whole research and development process. The hackers' use of their power was also a natural outgrowth of their original approach to hacking, since it implied that the person with the greatest knowledge about the computer's operations (and its flaws) had the right to use that knowledge as he wished.

The hackers who created and crashed those early time-sharing operating systems delighted in getting around any attempt to keep them away from the computer's resources. As far as they were concerned, any hacker who could find a way to circumvent or even destroy a barrier set up by the system operator wasn't at all obliged to keep from using his discovery – it was up to the system programmers and operators to patch up any holes in their software barriers.

The MAC hackers were in their heyday ten years earlier than the phone "phreaks" of the 1970s and almost twenty years before the Inner Circle was formed, but they had the same fundamental beliefs that modern-day hackers do: Nothing must prevent a hacker from knowing or learning as much as possible about a system's operation. Any software barrier to knowledge about a computer system was, and is, a challenge to all hackers.

THE SEVENTIES
HACKER

Our home computers can contact computers thousands of miles away because they can use devices called modems that enable them to "hear" and translate sounds sent over the nation's (and the world's) telephone communication system. Like all giant networks, however, the telephone system has its weak points, and one lies in the fact that a computer-to-computer hookup can occur without the knowledge of either the phone company or the invaded machine. This is the weakness that makes the telephone system and most computer systems vulnerable to hackers.

In the 1970s, before personal computers became as common as they are now, the telephone system itself was explored by a group of hackers who called themselves phone phreaks. The ethical and technical predecessors of today's hackers, the phone phreaks were anarchic "musicians" who delighted in using flutes, whistles, and any other sound generators that worked to enter and explore the worldwide telephone network.

The phone phreaks were far less organized and widespread than today's hackers are, and, in the beginning, none of them even knew of each other's existence. The cult itself came into being in the late 1960s, partly because of "phone hackers" at MIT and Stanford, where there were large computer centers and nests of hackers, and partly because of a brilliant young man in Tennessee named Joe Engressia.

Joe was the first phone phreak to achieve media notoriety, when a 1971 *Esquire* magazine article told the world about him and his cohorts. Like many other early phone phreaks, Joe is blind. He was only twenty-two when the article was published, but he had been tweaking the phone system since the age of eight. Telephones had always fascinated him, and Joe also happens to be one of those rare individuals who are born with perfect pitch. One day, by accident, he discovered how this gift could help him manipulate some of the most sophisticated and widespread technology in the world.

He was dialing recorded messages, partly because it was the only way he knew of to call around the world for free, and partly because it was a favorite pastime. He was whistling while listening to a recorded announcement when suddenly the recording clicked off. Someone with less curiosity might have assumed it was just one of those weird things the telephone company does to you, but Joe had an idea. He fooled around with some other numbers and discovered that he could switch off any recorded message by whistling a certain tone.

He called the local telephone company and asked why tape recorders stopped working when he whistled into the telephone. He didn't fully understand the explanation that was given to him at the time (remember, he was only eight years old), but it sounded as though he had stumbled into a whole new world of things to do and explore. And to a blind eight-year-old, an easily explored world, no farther away than his telephone, was, indeed, an intriguing discovery.

Joe was able to control some of the telephone company's global switching network – which is what he had stumbled upon with his whistling – because of a decision American Telephone & Telegraph (AT&T) made sometime in the 1950s. Their long-term, irreversible, multibillion-dollar decision was to base their long-distance switching on a series of specific, audible tones called a multifrequency system. The multifrequency system (known to phreaks as "MF") is a way for numbers that designate switching paths to be transmitted as tones similar to the sounds touch-tone phones make. Certain frequencies are used to find open lines, to switch from local to long-distance trunks, and, essentially, to do most of the jobs a human operator is able to do.

Undoubtedly, the decision-makers at AT&T did not give a moment's thought to the possibility that the system might someday fall before a blind eight-year-old with perfect pitch, but Joe found that he could maneuver his way through the system by whistling that one specific tone at the right time. His motivation was not to steal free telephone calls, but to find his way around the network and to learn how to extend his control over it.

Joe explored for years, but he never thought of himself as an enemy of the telephone system. He loved the system. His dream was to work for the telephone company someday, and he often tried to tell the company about bugs he discovered in the system. But he finally ran afoul of his intended employer when he was caught whistling up phone calls for fellow college students.

The publicity surrounding Joe's case had an unfortunate (for the telephone company) side effect: It led to the creation of the phone-phreak network. Soon after the story hit the papers, Joe began to get calls from all over the country. Some of the callers were blind, most were young, and all of them had one thing in common: an enormous curiosity about the telephone system. Joe put his callers in touch with one another, and these scattered experimenters soon found that they had stumbled upon several different ways to use the MF system as the ticket to a world of electronic globe-trotting.

Joe Engressia may have been the "phounding phather" of the phone phreaks, but just as one discovery often leads to another and another, it soon happened that someone else discovered a very large error made by the Bell Telephone System in 1954. The Bell System's technical journal had published a complete description of the multi-frequency system, including the specific frequencies and descriptions of how the frequencies were used.

Once the frequencies became public knowledge, phreaks began to use pipe organs, flutes, and tape recorders to create the tones that gave them control over the telecommunications network. And then came the ultimate irony: The news spread that a simple toy whistle included as a giveaway in boxes of Cap'n Crunch cereal produced a pure 2600-cycle tone if one of the holes in the whistle was taped shut. Using the whistle at just the right point in the process of making a connection, phreaks could call each other whenever and wherever they wanted without having to pay the phone company.

One of the more curious and inventive phreaks using the Cap'n Crunch whistle was John Draper, a young Air Force technician stationed overseas. Draper used the whistle for free calls to his friends in the United States. He was interested in the way this bizarre tool worked, so he began experimenting with the system and found that he could use the whistle and his knowledge of the switching network to route his calls in peculiar ways.

He began by calling people who worked inside the telephone system. They weren't aware that he was an outsider, so he was able to start gathering "intelligence." Soon, he was calling Peking and Paris, and routing calls to himself around the world. He set up massive clandestine conference calls that phreaks around the world could join and drop out of at will. Soon, he became known to the phreak underground as Cap'n Crunch.

Cap'n Crunch soon found out from other electronically minded phreaks that it was possible to build specially tuned electronic-tone generators that could reproduce the MF frequencies. A few electronic wizards began to circulate the generators, which were first known as

"MF boxes" because they reproduced the multifrequency tones, and later came to be called "blue boxes," as they are today.

The number of phreaks grew, and as they added their own discoveries to the collection of phreak knowledge, the cult's power to manipulate the system steadily increased. Then, in October 1971, the whole underground scene, from Joe Engressia to Cap'n Crunch, became well known to the outside world. *Esquire* magazine published "Secrets of the Little Blue Box" by Ron Rosenbaum, a journalist who had encountered the top phreaks of the time. Cap'n Crunch was characterized somewhat romantically in Rosenbaum's piece as a roving prankster who drove the author around in his specially equipped van, pausing frequently at public telephones to phone locations around the world: the American embassy in Moscow, a group of blind teenage phreaks in Canada, a public telephone in Trafalgar Square.

After the article was published (though not as a direct result), Crunch was arrested twice, convicted, and ended up spending four months at the federal prison in Lompoc, California in 1976, and two at Northampton State Prison in Pennsylvania in 1977. While he was in prison, several mob-connected inmates tried to enlist him in a commercial blue-box venture. Draper/Crunch declined. The convicts broke his back and knocked out his front teeth.

After he left prison, Draper quit phreaking and decided to start programming. An old friend by the name of Steve Wozniak seemed to be doing pretty well with a piece of hardware he called the Apple and Draper started writing software for Apple Computer. He developed a word-processing program known as EasyWriter and gained another niche in the technological Hall of Fame in 1981, when EasyWriter was selected as the first word-processing program available for the IBM PC. Now, Cap'n Crunch makes a legitimate living under a new handle, Cap'n Software.

TAP During his trial, John Draper claimed (and still claims) that his interest in phreaking was strictly devoted to learning about the workings of complex, worldwide communication-switching networks. There were other phreaks, though, of a more political mind, who saw this method of technological trespassing as a tool for spreading anarchy, and one

32

radical branch of the phreak fraternity grew out of the political group of the late sixties and early seventies known as the Yippies.

On May Day, 1971, the founding Yippie, Abbie Hoffman, and a phone phreak who used the handle Al Bell started a subversive publication, called the Youth International Party Line, which focused on information about cracking the phone network. A few years later, its name was changed to Technological Assistance Program (TAP), when the technological phreaks separated from their more politically oriented counterparts. TAP was purely anarchist. Through it, phreaks learned how to make plastic explosives, how to obtain phony birth certificates and illicit airline tickets, and how to abuse credit cards. It published circuit diagrams of blue boxes, and its members specialized in gaining and trading hard-to-get phone numbers – the Vatican, for example, or the Kremlin. TAP even secured the phone number of the American Embassy in Teheran after it was seized by students during the "hostage crisis" of 1980, posted the number, and invited phreaks to call the Embassy to "tell off" the revolutionary guards.

In the late 1970s the phreak who had been most closely associated with TAP also became a well-known hacker with the aliases Richard Cheshire and Cheshire Catalyst. Often employed as a computer and communications consultant by large corporations who are unaware of his secret identity, Cheshire has a widespread, carefully cultivated network of cohorts inside the telephone company and other institutions. Avoiding what he calls "dark-side hacking" that results in damage to data, Cheshire claims that there are some kinds of information that even TAP will not publish. For example, Cheshire once told a friend of mine: "A few years ago, before the *Progressive* magazine actually published the plans for making a hydrogen bomb, we were approached by someone who had similar plans. I decided that anything like the hydrogen bomb, which has the capability of destroying the phone network, is not in our interests."

Cheshire also mentioned an incident in which a hacker he knew stumbled upon the data-processing facilities of a top-secret American seismic station in Iceland, a facility responsible for monitoring Soviet nuclear testing. The hacker got out as soon as he realized where he was – "We try to stay away from that stuff," Cheshire said. He also remarked, "I once invited the CIA to attend a public lecture of mine, and there were a couple of guys at that talk, seated toward the back, who definitely turned a couple of shades of green when I told about that Icelandic station."

THE EIGHTIES
HACKER

Those were the days when computers were still too few and far between to gain the interest of telecommunicating hackers. But during the mid- to late-1970s, phone phreaking overlapped, and gradually merged with, the birth of the microcomputer industry. I'm sure that most of the Inner Circle would have been phone phreaks, if computers hadn't been there to lure them away, but beginning in 1975 and 1976, electronics technology and the development of packaged software began their headlong race into the future – one led by many of today's top hardware and program developers, some of whom have admittedly turned their attentions from blue boxes to big business in the years between.

By the early 1980s, hackers were starting to come out of the woodwork. Many people who already had an interest in computers were now starting to learn about the rapidly advancing field of telecommunications. Even more people were just becoming interested in computers. Mainframe computers began springing up all over the place, making hacking much more worthwhile than ever before. Personal computers were taking over the "offices of the future," their prices started dropping, and more and better programs appeared. The machines themselves became faster and more powerful by the day. IBM entered the fray with its Personal Computer and "legitimized" the industry for conservative onlookers.

Microcomputers found their way into homes, schools, and offices everywhere. The Inner Circle was formed and grew strong, and, between the middle of 1981 and the end of 1982, the population of hackers exploded to at least three times its former level.

Along with these developments, telecommunications became a big part of the computing life. Modems became smaller, faster, and smarter. Information networks sprang up everywhere, offering dial-up facts and figures on everything from the stock market to the latest in biochemical abstracts. And during this time, hackers were busy. So much so that some began to attract the attention of journalists and law-enforcement officials.

The telecommunications network at this time was a wonderland for hackers: big, exotic, complicated computers were a touch-tone away; bulletin-board systems (or BBSs) were set up for everyone from people seeking dates to school teachers. Hackers "met" other hackers via private and semiprivate bulletin boards. They exchanged tips, accounts, and phone numbers, and they learned who was good and who was not so good.

Then, the movie *WarGames* was released. Most hackers did not like the movie, but no matter how we felt about it, this film became a landmark in hacking history: Many, many people decided to try hacking on the basis of what they saw (or thought they saw) in *WarGames*. Handles like Warmonger, and esoteric references to Joshua (a key name in the movie), began to appear with distressing frequency. In fact, about seven or eight months after *WarGames* was released, the system operator of one bulletin-board system I knew of told me that he had perhaps 290 users, of whom only about 40 had been involved in telecommunications for much more than half a year.

At about the same time, and probably for the same cinematic reason, many other people began to become concerned about hacking. On the basis of one implausible, overly dramatized film, people began editorializing about hackers, and government agencies rushed to see whether their systems had been compromised. The FBI took an interest. Hackers were caught, their exploits publicized, and their computer equipment confiscated. Cases were taken to court, in the United States and elsewhere, and questions arose: Was hacking a threat or a nuisance? A crime or a lesser offense? Punishable? And if so, to what extent?

One post-*WarGames* group that got quite a lot of publicity was a group of Wisconsin teenagers who called themselves the 414s, after a local area code. Joseph B. Treaster, a staff reporter for *The New York Times* who has covered many recent hacker-related stories, interviewed one of the group shortly after they were apprehended by the FBI.

The 414s

According to the interview, the 414s had erased a few files in an attempt to cover their hacking tracks. They later discovered that they had erased a file incorrectly and were unable to correct the situation. This was bad enough from the Inner Circle's point of view, but worse yet was the fact that the damaged file was in a computer at the Sloan-Kettering Cancer Center in New York. The idea that technological vandals could, intentionally or otherwise, erase information at a cancer research and treatment center was one of the aspects of the case that everyone, including the Inner Circle, found appalling.

Another computer that these hackers compromised was located at the nuclear weapons research facility at Los Alamos, New Mexico. I am certain that the security people at Los Alamos are among the minority of computer-system administrators who are absolutely certain to keep their most sensitive systems physically sealed from telephone access. Still, it is unsettling to think that a computer belonging to any such facility – even a computer that has deliberately been made accessible to research scientists – can be penetrated by a group of mischief-seeking teenagers.

CHAPTER THREE

A Look at Computers

Aside from handles, private bulletin boards, accounts, and special phone numbers, a high-level hacker's world is made up of operating systems, programs, and machine code. If you don't know a VAX from a modem, or ASCII from an operating system, don't worry. While the technicalities can be very complicated, the concepts behind computers and the way they function are simple and very logical. To be a hacker, you would need to know much more than this book could teach you. To know about hacking, on the other hand, you don't need any more information than this "tutorial" chapter will cover.

What is telecommunications? These days, it's usually the ability to use the telephone network to connect your home or business computer to a computer located somewhere else. Maybe the other computer is another home computer that belongs to a friend or colleague. Maybe it is a minicomputer or a mainframe that is located at your home office

TELECOMMU-NICATIONS IN GENERAL

across the country. Or maybe it is a public-access computer, such as the ones operated by THE SOURCE, CompuServe, Dow Jones, and other such services. In any case, the means you use to communicate with that other computer is a small device, called a modem, that connects your computer with the telephone system and, through that system, to the computer at the other end of the line.

That's telecommunications: two computers "talking" to each other via their own translators, or modems. They need the modems, because computer "speech" is in the form of electrical impulses, rather than sound, and it is also very exact and very fast. The modems enable computers to use the voice-based, inexact (by computer standards), and relatively slow (again, by computer standards) phone system to transfer data at speeds of up to thousands of characters per minute. Since computers have no idea of who might be impersonating whom over the phone system, modems also enable hackers to connect with, and explore, some fascinating machines.

In the past few years, the technology of home telecommunications has been racing ahead like a horse in the Kentucky Derby. Although many people may not be sure about what goes on behind the scenes, almost everyone realizes that the mysterious "system" where sysops and hackers play their equally mysterious games is vitally important in the world as it exists today. Whether you know or care about telecommunications, everything from your birth certificate to your checkbook balance and your Social Security account is coded, stored, and transmitted through the national and, sometimes, the international communications network. The groceries you buy, the newspapers you read, the plane reservations for your vacation – all rely on telecommunications and computer systems in some way.

Through telecommunications, we have the ability to transmit and record information much faster than ever before. Airline reservations are made on the spot. Funds are transferred within a few hours. Corporate files and interoffice memos no longer depend on the post office – they can be sent across the country as quickly as they can be sent across town.

All of this means that a great deal of information – sometimes very valuable information – is either traveling from one computer to another through the telephone network, or it is accessible to a computer that can use a telephone and a modem. And, as hackers know, this vast, intriguing network can be penetrated by a $200 computer and a $150 modem.

All computers are run by devices called *central processors,* which are the master control devices that oversee all of the other functions of the computer. Processors are composed of the often-mentioned chips designed, developed, and produced by the electronics wizards of the industry. Processors are also the pieces of a computer's "innards" that use numbers to help you turn your computer into a word processor, a spreadsheet generator, or a video-game player. Altogether, a computer's processor(s) and associated hardware are known as the *central processing unit,* or *CPU.*

Given this fundamental "brainpower," you would think that it would be easy to categorize computers according to how "smart" they are. To some extent, they can be grouped by the strength and speed of their processors but, as I said earlier, the technicalities can be complicated and, in the end, this basic defining characteristic becomes intertwined with function, storage capacity, and other factors so that groupings become as much a matter of opinion as they are a matter of fact. As far as we are concerned, however, computers can be divided into five basic groups: microcomputers, minicomputers, superminicomputers, mainframes, and supercomputers.

A microcomputer is the smallest and least powerful of the five types of computers. It is usually defined as a computer that is run by a single microprocessor, and a microprocessor is a central processor, or CPU, on a single chip – an ultraminiaturized circuit that is so small it would get lost if you dropped it on a shag rug. A microcomputer almost always also qualifies as a *personal computer,* because all of its resources are dedicated entirely to one person at a time. In other words, it cannot be used by several different people simultaneously.

According to these definitions, the Apple II, the IBM PC family, the Commodore 64, and the Timex-Sinclair 1000 are microcomputers.

TYPES OF COMPUTERS

Microcomputers

39

On the other hand, and here is where some of the fuzziness I mentioned comes into play, not all of these machines are necessarily personal computers. The IBM PC, PC XT, and, especially, the new PC AT can all easily be set up to divide their resources among several to many people so, depending on function, these microcomputers may or may not be "personal" as well.

Minicomputers   The next step in the computer hierarchy is the minicomputer, which is almost always used as a business computer. Minicomputers are usually larger and more expensive than microcomputers, and they have the ability to time-share, or divide their resources among dozens of users. While the main memory of most microcomputers is measured in tens or hundreds of kilobytes, the main memory of some minicomputers can be in the multiple megabyte range – ten to a hundred times larger.

Main memory is a very important point when talking about or categorizing computers, because the power of a computer depends entirely on the kinds of programs it can run. Powerful programs are complex programs, and complex programs require a large amount of main memory to function. That, in fact, is one reason hackers like to gain access to minicomputers, and even bigger machines: Suddenly, they have the freedom to use far more computing power than a microcomputer can possibly provide.

Minicomputers cost anywhere from $5000 to $1,000,000, but most are in the $20,000 to $60,000 range. Generally, computers like Sage V, Data General's Nova, and Hewlett-Packard's HP-3000 are thought of as minicomputers.

Supermini-computers   As technology advances and new computers become more powerful, the computers that a year or two ago were considered powerful and expensive become more common. Distinctions blur, and what used to be A now becomes B. That is essentially what is happening in the minicomputer category, and some "minis" that are used primarily by large businesses now qualify as superminicomputers because their main memory and processing speed are substantially greater than those of regular minicomputers. Superminicomputers can cost as much as several million dollars, and some even have more information storage capacity than the mainframe computers that are one step higher in the computer hierarchy. The VAX you read about in the story at the beginning of this book is generally considered a superminicomputer. There is another one, called a Prime, and both IBM and Digital Equipment Corporation also manufacture superminicomputers.

Mainframes are the machines that usually come to mind when you think "big computer." They are the ones with such names as IBM-370, DEC-20, and Prime 750. As a general rule, mainframes are the most powerful computers in widespread commercial use. They can almost always handle more than one hundred users at a time, they are faster, and they can usually store more information than a minicomputer.

Mainframes

Supercomputers are at the very top of the heap. They are the most powerful computers in existence, and most hackers would love to find one. At the moment, however, there are only a few – the Cray and Cyber computers and a few Japanese counterparts – that qualify as supercomputers. They are used by organizations, such as NASA and the Pentagon, that have really high-powered computing requirements. Supercomputers are extremely fast, and one of their main features is their ability to perform some operations simultaneously, rather than one by one as all other computers do.

Supercomputers

Any computer, no matter how powerful its hardware might be, is useless without a program to run. You are probably familiar with word-processing programs, spreadsheet programs, database programs, and game programs. These contain instructions that turn your computer into a particular type of servant. But to allow your computer to use these special-purpose programs in the first place, you need a special control program known as an operating system.

OPERATING SYSTEMS

Every computer needs an operating system. Without one, the machine will never do anything: never check the keyboard for input, never display anything on the screen, never remember anything for you, never forget anything for you, never impassively tell you FILE NOT FOUND.

In the world of microcomputers, there are several major operating systems, such as CP/M (which stands for Control Program for Microcomputers) and MS-DOS (which stands for Microsoft Disk Operating System). Larger computers use other operating systems. Prime computers, for example, use one called Primos ("os" is often used as an abbreviation for "operating system"). On a VAX, the operating system is most likely to be VMS. On DEC-10s and DEC-20s, an operating system called TOPS-20 is often used.

All of these operating systems function in different ways, but regardless of the computer they run on, their job is the same: They are responsible for telling the computer what to do when it first comes to life and for making it able to run other programs.

How They Are Used

The most basic part of an operating system is always in the computer in special memory that isn't erased even when the power is turned off. This basic part usually initializes the computer's memory and tells the computer how to get the main operating system, which it does by loading the program, usually from disk, into main memory. Once the operating system is loaded, the computer is capable of receiving, displaying, storing, retrieving, and transmitting information, and of performing the calculations that a computer is expected to perform.

When the operating system is ready to get to work, it gives the user a *prompt,* a visual signal that tells the person it is waiting for input from the keyboard. On a microcomputer, the first input is usually a command of some sort that tells the computer what to do next. On large time-sharing systems, the first keystrokes are usually the user's account name and private password, which tell the computer who is *logging on* and give the system a chance to verify the person's right to use computer time. (This is the first level of computer security, by the way, and hackers are often required to breach this security in order to use the computer.)

The prompt itself can be any symbol that the system programmer cares to choose, as long as it can be displayed on a video screen. Most prompts are either one or two characters long. Some include some type of information, such as the time or date, or an indication of what part of the computer the user is connected to at the moment. But usually, prompts are short and sweet, like the famous A> often used on microcomputers.

Regardless of the type of prompt, once the initial command or log-on sequence is accepted by the operating system, the computer is at the disposal of the user. The operating system "knows" that someone wants to do something, and as long as that something is within its or another program's abilities, the operating system continues to pay attention to the keyboard, translating each line of text that the user enters into numeric codes that the computer can understand. This is the reason why we can type in words that almost seem like normal English – words like ERASE FILE or COPY FILE – instead of a seemingly endless string of random-looking numbers.

Because of the jobs it does and the equipment it controls, the operating system is at the core of any computer's ability to do anything. Complex, coldly logical, and endlessly fascinating to a hacker, the operating system is the link between user and computer. It is also where many major security procedures are implemented – or thwarted.

HOW
COMPUTERS
COMMUNICATE

Like people, computers often speak different "dialects." Unlike people, however, they cannot communicate unless they use *exactly* the same "words." By all this, I'm not referring to programming languages, such as BASIC or COBOL. I mean something a lot more fundamental: the coding that is used to represent words, numbers, commas, quote marks, and every other piece of information that computers of any size must handle.

That coding, or common language, is known as ASCII (short for American Standard Code for Information Interchange). ASCII is simply an agreed-upon system for converting computer data into 128 alphabetic and numeric characters, as well as punctuation marks and mathematical symbols. This system allows information to be sent to and from totally incompatible computer systems. Just over 90 of these characters are visible; the others are known as *control characters* – in other words, characters, such as those representing "carriage return" or "tab," that normally don't appear on the screen but are supposed to "control" a computer.

Technical as it may sound, ASCII is really very simple. It assigns a specific number to each of the 128 characters it recognizes as valid. For example, the ASCII code number for the capital letter A is 65; for a period, it is 46, and for a lowercase a, it is 97. The transmitting computer simply translates everything it is sending into this ASCII code, and as long as the receiving computer can "understand" ASCII, and no non-ASCII characters are included, everything is OK. Communication is assured and, using ASCII as a common language, the computers can send and receive information at very fast speeds.

0 and 1, the Magic Numbers

Now that we have computers speaking a common language – the language of numbers – the next step is to find out how they "think" of these numbers.

Every computer in the world, from the giants that send spaceships to the moon to the smallest game-playing home computer, shares a common denominator, a universal currency, the numbers 0 and 1. These two numbers are the famous *bits*, or binary digits. They are the only two digits used in the binary, or base-2, number system, just as 0 through 9 are the only ten digits in our familiar base-10 decimal system. Zero and one are very comfortable for computers to work with, because they can represent the two electrical states used by the machines – high and low voltage. And between them, the two binary digits can be combined in longer and longer groups to represent any conceivable number.

Computer people don't usually work with bits, though; they are too small. Instead, the most commonly used unit is a group of eight bits, called a *byte,* and is approximately the amount of information storage needed to specify one alphanumeric or control character. Larger groups of bytes are kilobytes (KB), or roughly one thousand bytes, and megabytes (MB), or about one million bytes. But all of these groupings still are multiples of 2, the binary digits 0 and 1.

If you own or use a microcomputer (or personal computer), you know about your computer's amount of RAM, or random access memory, and its disk-storage capacity – its ability to store information on either floppy or hard disks. On these computers, memory is measured in kilobytes, and disk storage is measured in kilobytes or megabytes.

44

Bits, bytes, kilobytes, or megabytes – in the end they all represent the same thing: numbers. Numbers that connect telephones, give orders to computers, record financial transactions, track rockets to the moon, and monitor nuclear missiles. All numbers, just numbers. When you say that computers process information, you are also saying that computers store and retrieve, add and subtract, send and receive various collections of numbers, all of which are stored as binary numbers and all of which are kept and made accessible as data files.

By using ASCII as a common language, computers can send and receive information at very fast speeds. When they communicate over a phone line, however, they must use modems and they must slow down considerably to allow for several intermediary steps. Instead of using a cable for direct computer-to-computer transmission, they must use a computer-to-modem-to-phone-to-modem-to-computer hookup. This communications relay is still much faster than many other communications technology now widely available, however, and in terms of spoken words, it can still be pretty fast.

In their work as "translators," modems do two things: MOdulate and DEModulate – that's how they got their name. Essentially what happens is that the sending computer's modem converts the information into a series of sound impulses that are able to travel over a telephone wire; this is the modulation process. On the other end, the receiving computer's modem translates the sounds back into the binary data that the computer can understand; this is the demodulation process.

The speed at which computers and modems send and receive data is measured in *baud,* or bits per second. Most modems cannot communicate over the phone lines at more than 1200 baud, and quite a few cannot handle any more than 300 baud. At 300 baud, information is moving to or from a computer at the rate of about 30 characters per second; at 1200 baud, it is moving about four times as fast. In contrast, when computers are connected directly, they usually transmit data at 4800, 9600, or 19200 baud when using ASCII. At 19200 baud, information is moving at just about 20,000 characters per second.

COMMUNI-
CATIONS
TECHNOLOGY

Modems

Terminals   A terminal is a piece of equipment used for communicating with a computer. A terminal can either be connected directly to a computer by a cable or, if the terminal is equipped with a modem, it can be anywhere in the world. In addition, a terminal can be either "smart" or "dumb." A smart terminal has a microprocessor and is thus capable of independent "thought," whereas a dumb terminal has no micro-processor and is simply a device for sending and receiving information. Now, to make life a little more complicated, there's one more either/or: A terminal, smart or dumb, either may or may not be associated with a modem. Let's clarify matters with a few examples:

A dumb terminal with no modem is a sending and receiving device only and must be connected ("hard-wired") to a computer by means of a cable.

A dumb terminal with a modem is still a sending and receiving device, but it can be anywhere, because the modem enables it to use a telephone to access the computer. A dumb terminal with a modem is the device I used in my first attempts at hacking.

A smart terminal with no modem is capable of communicating with a computer, as long as it is connected to the larger machine by a cable, *and* it is capable of processing information on its own. It is often a microcomputer.

A smart terminal with a modem is capable of communicating with a computer from any location that gives it access to the telephone system and, again, it is capable of processing information on its own. A microcomputer equipped with a modem can also be considered to be a smart terminal.

When a computer allows a terminal to access it from a remote location, it treats that remote terminal just as if there were a cable connecting them directly, in the same room. As long as the remote terminal is connected to a communications *port*, or channel, through which information can enter and leave the system, the computer neither knows nor cares where the terminal is physically located.

NETWORKS   When several computers are connected to one another via permanent long-distance communication links, they are parts of a *network*. The first computer network, and one that is still explored today by many hackers, is called ARPANET and was created in the late 1960s by researchers working on projects for the U.S. Defense Department. ARPANET was a boon to these researchers, because it enabled them to communicate and share information, even though they and their computers were located many thousands of miles apart.

In the '70s and '80s, the ideas that were first developed by the Defense Department began to be applied to commercial networks in which business or research computers used the same kind of technology used in ARPANET. With the growing use of both large and small computers, and the need for people other than computer specialists to make use of computer resources from remote locations, public-network technology (and the public-network business) developed very rapidly. Today, it's probably safe to say that more than 100,000 large computers are connected to telephone lines.

A public network, like the one in the diagram, can be defined as an alternate route for your telecommunications data. The company that owns the network has modems in certain cities that it selects for local access to the network. Then, the network company routes your

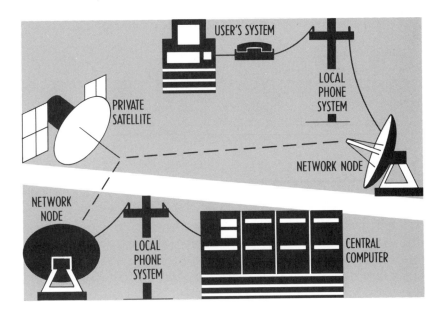

call through its own long-distance service, so that you end up within a local distance of the computer you are calling. The phone system itself is actually used only for local calls, so the result is that if, for example, you live in Indianapolis, you can call a network computer in Boston without having to make a direct, long-distance phone connection.

THE HUMAN NETWORK

So far, we've covered a great deal about machines and operating systems. Now we can put them in perspective by seeing how they are related to the people who use and run them: Let's take a look at the human side of the connection.

Computer security is based on the idea that certain information stored in the computer should be made available only to people with a "need to know," and that measures must be taken to prevent unauthorized people from using information that they either cannot, for technical reasons, or should not, for other reasons, have access to.

There was a time in the history of computers when there was no such custom of preventing particular users from using particular files. The practice started with the appearance of the first time-sharing computers. Before time-sharing, computers were capable of running only one program at a time, so only one person could use the computer at any one time.

The Beginnings of Computer Security

When time-sharing programs made it possible for many people to run many programs at the same time, the operating system suddenly had to keep track of many more people. To make this informational housekeeping easier to do, the operators of those systems assigned each user a unique *user name* that identified him or her to the computer. When people wanted to use the computer, they would *log on* by entering their user names; in this way the system was able to tell the difference between one user and another. When people had finished using the computer, they would *log off* to tell the computer they were done, and make room for another user to log on in their place.

This system worked well, but it quickly became necessary to make sure that one user could not modify or erase the files belonging to another user, so the people who designed these first time-sharing systems put a program into the operating system that would allow users to change or delete only their own files. In effect, this program turned the computer from a kind of open file cabinet into one with more restricted access. Private passwords were born, both to protect people's files and, because computers were still pretty expensive machines to run, to keep people from using each other's computer time.

In order to use a time-sharing computer, people now logged on by entering both a correct account name and a correct account password. The account/password security device became the main security feature of most time-sharing systems, and it is still widely used today. Few, if any, time-sharing systems work differently. Some systems add additional security measures to the account/password method but, so far, no new methods have replaced the tried-and-true account/password combination.

Regulating access to accounts was the first, but not the only, level of security that was created with the first time-sharing systems. The administrators of those early systems were also concerned about the amount of *power* given to each account. Power in this sense is the ability to manipulate other files.

Levels of Security

When the first account names and passwords were created, new programs were also created to exercise control over the files in the system. These were programs that could tell the system to accept new users, deny access to old users, erase files, reset passwords, and take care of other such "supervisory" chores. Naturally, these new programs also opened the door to potential chaos if everyone could use them, so these program files were kept away from the users and reserved for the *system operators* who were responsible for overseeing the entire system.

Eventually, the allocation of power over computer files led to the development of a user hierarchy that is still in existence today. This hierarchy is based on the fact that a wide range of people with a wide range of computer-related abilities may all need access to the resources of a single large computer. For example, programmers know more about computers than people who use these machines only as word processors, so programmers need more power to manipulate certain files. Similarly, system accountants need access to files that programmers have no need to see or change. And over all these others, there is the system operator who has the power to run the entire system. This is the hierarchy that hackers seek to climb whenever they begin to explore a new computer.

The System Operator

Although the story of Al and George, the MegaCar system operators, and the discussion of computer security in this chapter may have led you to believe that system operators, or sysops, must be enormously powerful creatures sitting alone at the top of the computer hierarchy, you would be giving them both too much and too little credit by thinking of them in such terms.

The job of "system operator" is less easy to define than, say, the job of "doctor" or "plumber." These latter professions imply a certain amount of specific education and training. A system operator, on the other hand, can be anyone from a person who has worked with computers for twenty years but doesn't necessarily know a great deal about them, to someone with a 4.0 average and a degree in computer science from MIT. A system operator may teach computer science at MIT, or be a high-school student working during the summer.

For the most part, though, system operators do know quite a bit about computers, and for one main reason: Very few people apply for the job, and a large number of those who do apply, especially in a university environment, have already been involved with computers for awhile. Many of these people see the job as a great opportunity to play with multimillion dollar equipment – *legally.*

A system operator is often called an "operator" and, in fact, performs a job similar to that of a telephone operator. A system operator takes care of the system and, if a user needs to do something special or has a problem, the operator has the power to override the system's security to help out – just as a telephone operator can credit your account if you call a wrong number. Most of the system operator's tasks are very ordinary, such as changing a disk or moving a reel of tape. And, usually, a system operator sits around the computer room drinking coffee and doing crossword puzzles. Then again, he may sit around reading computer books or he may even play with the system. It all depends on who he is, and where he works.

Regardless of his background, however, as you can see, a system operator's need of power is not the need for some godlike ability to give and to take away. The power is much closer to a hacker's interests, because it is the power to control a computer.

Where Hackers Fit in

A hacker is someone who wants to know anything and everything about computer systems. In order to gain that knowledge, he must be able to climb the user pyramid. This is how it often happens:

In an institution such as a large business or a university, there is a large community of computer users, many of whom use only the word-processing, file-storage, or communication capabilities provided by the system. They know little about the complexities of the system itself, unless they happen to be interested for other reasons. These people are the users who are at the bottom of the computer hierarchy.

Some users are programmers who know the computer's own language, so they know more about the computer than the people on the bottom level. Moving higher up the hierarchy, there are some programmers, called system programmers, who know more than other programmers because they know how the computer's operating system works. And, because there is usually a need to regulate how much power the different users are given, there is almost always a system operator at the top.

On most computer systems, there is a list of anywhere from seven to a hundred "rights" that an account on the system can have. Obviously, the more and better rights an account has, the more powerful it is. The system operator has all of these rights, whereas a typical user may have only one or two. When a hacker manages to secure an account on a new system and asks for information that he would find useful or interesting, the computer responds with INSUFFICIENT PRIVILEGE if the information requested is not within the rights of that account. Such a response is guaranteed to challenge a high-level hacker, because he has probably started off with a very low-level account – possibly even lower than the ones given to typical users.

From then on, the hacker will try to gain more power on the system, either by granting more rights to his account or, more likely, by gaining other accounts that already have more rights. In the first instance, the hacker will almost always have to trick either the system operator or the system itself into giving more rights to an existing account. If, on the other hand, he decides to go after accounts owned by other people, he can try to trick the system, the operator, or the user. As you will see in later chapters, there are many ways a hacker goes about hacking. But if, as was true of the Inner Circle, he seeks knowledge about the system and wants to gain more and better ways of exploring the computer, the hacker's goal is an account with as much power as that of the system operator.

HELP IS WHERE YOU FIND IT

Now that we've looked at computers, computer security, and computer use in general, it might be a good idea to take a look at a specific computer and see how it can be used.

Up until now, perhaps you have thought that computers always talked in strange languages or used pulsing lights or long strings of numbers. On a very simple level, all computers do, indeed, operate in a fashion similar to that. On the level at which computers interact with most people, however, computers are quite simple to deal with.

Take this next example, for instance. Let's assume that you and I are just learning about computers and have no idea how to work with them. We are learning, not on a microcomputer, as most people do, but on a superminicomputer, a VAX, that typically would cost over half a million dollars and be used by a medium-sized or large company. We log on (the authorized way) by typing in an account name and password. Here is what we see:

$

Hmm. Not much there, so when in doubt, ask for help!
We try asking for help....

$ **help**

The system quickly responds....

Information available:
ACCOUNTING	ALLOCATE	ANALYZE
APPEND	ASSIGN	ATTACH
BACKUP	BASIC	BLISS

CANCEL	CC	CLOSE
COBOL	CONTINUE	CONVERT
COPY	CORAL	CREATE
DBO	DDL	DEALLOCATE
DEASSIGN	DEBUG	DECK
DEFINE	DELETE	DEPOSIT
DIFFERENCES	DIRECTORY	DISMOUNT
DUMP	EDIT	EOD
EOJ	Errors	EXAMINE
EXIT	FDL	FORTRAN
GOTO	HELP	IF
INITIALIZE	INQUIRE	JOB
Lexical	LIBRARY	LINK
Login	LOGOUT	MACRO
MAIL	MCR	MERGE
MESSAGE	MONITOR	MOUNT
ON	OPEN	PASCAL
PASSWORD	PATCH	PHONE
PLI	PRINT	Procedure
PURGE	Queues	READ
RENAME	REPLY	REQUEST
RMS	RTL	RUN
RUNOFF	SEARCH	SET
SHOW	SORT	SPAWN
Specify	SPSS	SPSS-X
SPSSX	START	STOP
SUBMIT	Symbol_Assign	SYNCHRONIZE
System	TECO	TIME
TSP	TYPE	UNLOCK
WAIT	WRITE	

Hmm ... let's see ... well, we have heard of BASIC before — it's supposed to be pretty simple....

Topic? **basic**

BASIC

Invokes the VAX-11 BASIC compiler....

Format:

BASIC [source-file [, ...]]

If you supply one or more file specifications, BASIC compiles the source file(s). If you do not supply a file specification, you enter the BASIC environment and receive the Ready prompt.

If you separate source file specifications with commas, BASIC compiles each module separately and produces multiple object

53

files. If you separate source file specifications with plus signs (+), BASIC appends the files and produces a single object file.

Additional information available:
Qualifiers

/ANSI_STANDARD	/AUDIT	/CHECK
/CROSS	/DEBUG	/DECIMAL_SIZE
/DOUBLE	/FLAG	/INTEGER_SIZE
/LINES	/LIST	/MACHINE
/OBJECT	/REAL_SIZE	/ROUND
/SCALE	/SHOW	/SINGLE
/SYNTAX_CHECK	/TYPE_DEFAULT	/VARIANT
/WARNING	/WORD	RELEASE_NOTES

That looks complicated so let's go to BASIC firsthand....

BASIC Subtopic? **<return>**

Topic? **<return>**

$ basic

VAX-11 BASIC V2.2

Ready

Hmm ... not much to do but ask for help again....

help

HELP

The HELP command displays on-line information about BASIC statements, commands, directives, functions, conventions, and other topics. Type HELP to see a list of topics. Then enter a subtopic for more information. If you type a question mark in response to the prompt for a topic, BASIC displays the list of available topics.

Additional information available:

ARRAYS	CHARACTER	COMMANDS
COMMENTS	CONSTANTS	CONVENTIONS
DATA_TYPES	DIRECTIVES	ERRORS
EXPRESSIONS	FUNCTIONS	HELP
IMMEDIATE	LABELS	LINE
MODIFIERS	QUALIFIERS	RELEASE_NOTES
STATEMENTS	VARIABLES	

Topic? **stat**

The whole word need not be entered. . . .

STATEMENTS

Statements assign values, perform I/O, transfer program control, and so forth. Program statements are associated with a line number and stored for later execution. A statement starting in the first column and having no line number is executed as an immediate mode statement. For additional information on immediate mode statements, type "HELP IMMEDIATE".

Statement modifiers are keywords that qualify or restrict a statement. For help on modifiers, type "HELP MODIFIERS".

Additional information available:

CALL	CHAIN	CHANGE
CLOSE	COMMON	DATA
DECLARE	DEF	DELETE
DIMENSION	END	EXIT
EXTERNAL	FIND	FNEND
FNEXIT	FOR	FREE
FUNCTION	FUNCTIONEND	FUNCTIONEXIT
GET	GOSUB	GOTO
IF	INPUT	ITERATE
KILL	LET	LINPUT
LSET	MAP	MARGIN
MAT	MOVE	NAME_AS
NEXT	NOMARGIN	ON
OPEN	OPTION	PRINT
PUT	RANDOMIZE	READ
RECORD	REM	REMAP
RESTORE	RESUME	RETURN
RSET	SCRATCH	SELECT
SLEEP	STOP	SUB
SUBEND	SUBEXIT	UNLESS
UNLOCK	UNTIL	UPDATE
WAIT	WHILE	

A lot of statements . . . let's see what it says about GOTO. . . .

STATEMENTS Subtopic? **goto**

STATEMENTS

GOTO

The GOTO statement transfers control to a specified line number or label.

Format

{ GO TO }

{ GOTO } target

Example.

20   GOTO 200

STATEMENTS Subtopic? <**return**>

Topic? <**return**>

Ready

And here we are again. . . .

The point of this example is to show that a typical expensive piece of computer equipment is *not* as difficult to operate as most people would think. Most systems in operation today make it possible for you to ask for help from just about any possible place. You can ask about a language, about the mass storage, in some cases about phone numbers to other computers. . . .

CHAPTER FOUR

Who Hacks and Why

It's Sunday night, and I'm in my room, deep into a hack. My eyes are on the monitor, and my hands are on the keyboard, but my mind is really on the operating system of a superminicomputer a thousand miles away – a supermini with an operating system that does a good job of tracking users, and that will show my activities in its user logs, unless I can outwit it in the few hours before the Monday-morning staff arrives for work.

The only light in the room comes from the green screen of my computer monitor and the small red lights on my modem. I turn and check the clock: 3:00 a.m. "Good," I think. "Three hours before I have to leave for school. Too bad I didn't have time to do any homework." Thoughts of school evaporate, and I return to my computer with the enthusiasm of a Super Bowl football player.

Eighteen hours ago, I managed to hack a password for this PDP 11/44. Now, I have only an hour or so left to alter the user logs. If I don't, the logs will lead the system operators to my secret account, and the hours of work it took me to get this account will be wasted. I've got to cover my tracks; I can only hope the company doesn't use printed copies of the logs. Those I can't change.

An hour passes and I begin to fear the worst . . . if only I had more time. But I realize that I'd best say goodbye to my account as I watch the first couple of users log on: ACCT004 – that one's all right, it's a low-level user's account. SYS01 – hmm . . . that's the sysop. The game's over, and I've only changed the log for one of the twenty-four accounts I looked into. I'd better stay home today and use my secret account until the system operators find me and remove it. I wonder how long it will take them to figure out that I'm here.

UNDER-STANDING HACKERS

Very few people, from the designers and operators of large systems to the investigators and law-enforcement officers who deal with hackers, understand *what* hackers are trying to do, much less *why* they're trying to do it. During my own trial, for example, the judge decided to postpone sentence until after I had undergone psychiatric evaluation.

What makes hackers hack? Why are they so dedicated? Why do they spend so much of their own time on other people's computer systems? And just what do they think they are trying to accomplish? It is not rare for a hacker to put in a sixty- or seventy-hour work week (without getting paid, of course). And these are not empty hours, filled by staring out the window. Hacking is a challenge and a game of wits, and during their work sessions, hackers are using all the skills and ingenuity they have developed. Hackers enjoy what they do.

Suppose *your* business or research computer system is the object of such a hacker's "affection." Obviously, you will be faced with a lot of dedicated, not to mention clandestine, effort. Depending on the kind of hacker who finds your system, you could also be faced with the potential for abuse and destruction of your programs and data.

Before you can find the right security countermeasures for your own computer system, you need to understand who your opponents are, and why they are testing your defenses. I am not qualified to discuss hackers in philosophical or psychological terms, but I can give you some practical answers to what is ultimately a practical problem: I can introduce you to hackers in general, and to several very different types of hackers I know about. Once you understand why these different types of hackers hack, it should be easier for you to recognize the different dangers they pose to unprotected or inadequately secured computer systems.

A better understanding of hackers will help you immeasurably on this ever-changing battlefield, because hackers will always be hackers. They'll always be probing your security, and for the same reasons they do so today. Even if hackers' techniques evolve far beyond their present tricks, or their personal equipment eventually dwarfs the capabilities of a multimillion-dollar IBM-370 mainframe, the person you will have to discover, identify, and handle in some way will be just like the hacker who may be on your system today.

From my years as a hacker, and from my years of communicating with other hackers, I think I can safely say that a typical hacker is in his teens or early twenties, and almost always someone whom people would call a "fast learner." He is either at a very advanced academic level, in a "gifted" program in school, moving at his own pace (in which case he doesn't really have the time to be a *good* hacker), or he is bored with school.

HACKER PROFILES

The teachers of hackers who are bored students might argue with my characterization of them as extremely fast learners. On the other hand, there was a time, not very long ago, during which about one percent of the U.S. population had computers; ninety-nine percent (or thereabouts) of hackers came from that time. Now, when there are millions of Apples, IBM PCs, Commodore 64s, and so forth, comparatively few new hackers are emerging. Aside from the obvious reasons, such as better mainframe security and more microcomputer software to choose from, I believe hackers are more motivated than most people, and that it is probably just this motivation that helps make anyone "bright," at least in his or her own field.

Just watch a high-level hacker at work on a subject that truly attracts his interest, and you'll see what he can do when he puts his mind to it. That subject – really a state of mind more than anything else – is hacking. A hacker can hack a minicomputer, a supermini, or a mainframe with anything from a $150 dumb terminal to a $7000 IBM personal computer system. (In most cases, the "smarter," more expensive system is just easier and more convenient to work with; it doesn't necessarily make hacking the target computer very much easier.)

I've also noticed that many hackers, when they "grow up," choose to work with computers as a profession, and usually turn out to be far more dedicated and knowledgeable than their non-hacker colleagues. This dedication is easy to understand once you realize that a universal trait among hackers is pride in the amount and quality of their knowledge – pride that, often enough, verges on arrogance. After all, if you have figured out how to crack a very difficult system, it is part of your nature as a good programmer to want to see if your method works. This is the reason that a large percentage of system operators have dabbled in hacking at one time or another. While hacking, I've talked to hundreds of system operators, and I'd estimate that probably seventy to eighty percent of them claim to have been hackers at some point in their lives. They love talking about such matters.

There is another important trait that is common to hackers: They all share an intense, compelling interest in computers. This common ground is the basis for the few unwritten rules that I mentioned in Chapter One: Never delete or alter information you cannot easily restore; never leave your (or any other hacker's) name on a computer; always try to obtain your own account information and do not exist as a parasite on the findings of other hackers.

Most hackers follow these rules most of the time, because:

≡ *They would like to keep the account information they went to so much trouble to get.*

≡ *They would like to stay out of legal trouble, if possible.*

≡ *They like computers and don't have any reason to cause trouble to them or for the people who run them.*

≡ *They love the elaborate, complex logic of computer systems. People who find pleasure in destroying data are not motivated by love of the system or by respect for other hackers.*

With this general information in mind, let's move on and take a closer look at each of five different types of hacker: the Novice, the Student, the Tourist, the Crasher, and the Thief.

Frequent references to the movie *WarGames,* mixed in with a few phrases like "Got any awesome numbers?" typify the Novice. These hackers are younger than most – maybe twelve to fourteen – so they often live off throw-away accounts from the more advanced Students I'll describe next. I would imagine that Novices think of hacking as play, or mischief-making, and not much more than that. Of all the different groups I'll describe, they are the ones most likely to be drawn by the image of hacking as a fun and somewhat "naughty" pursuit. I'm sure they enjoy playing with computers, but to them, hacking *is* play. It isn't (and maybe never will be) programming, assembly language, and operating systems.

The Novice

Novices are very unpredictable, because of their inexperience, and their population is rapidly growing, because of recent glamorous publicity, but for the most part they are "safe" in terms of reasonably secure computer systems. Assuming that Novices can get onto a system in the first place, they will usually just log on, type PLAY GAMES, WITHDRAW $20,000, and CATALOG or DIR (to see what sorts of file names the computer will display). Then they will most likely get bored and go off to play Super-Invaders or do their homework.

When caught and confronted by a system operator – or another hacker – a Novice will almost always announce himself quite clearly.

I know of one Novice who was detected by the Inner Circle while they were on a Prime computer. The unknown hacker was using an account belonging to a former employee, someone who had not had access to the Prime for several months, so the Inner Circle members were certain there was another hacker on the system. To find out who he was, and to test his capability, they used one of the operating system's special programs, one that allows two users to type messages to one another, to "break in" and send a specially worded message to the new hacker: MARC, IS THAT YOU? An experienced hacker would have sent them some ambiguous reply or tried to hide his identity in some way. Instead, they received: I AM NOT MARC. I'M A HACKER

HA HA HA! I'LL INITIALIZE YOUR HARD DRIVE IF YOU DON'T TAKE OFF!!!! They had contacted a Novice.

The Student   I considered myself a Student, and if someone had asked me why I was hacking, this is what I would have said:

"I come home after a typical day in school, wishing they would actually *teach* me something – get me interested. I throw my homework on the floor, flip on my terminal, and go over the list of accounts I've acquired. I have access to any of a dozen or so systems ranging from two-hundred-thousand-dollar college computers to multibillion-dollar corporate systems. I decide I'll start the day out with a DEC-10 in Nebraska... it has four or five games on it I like to play.

"If I decide I can stop work long enough to attend school, at best I am disappointed by the amount and level of anything I learn during those 'wasted' hours. More likely, though, I will complain about the repetition of it all: 'You told us that yesterday,' 'This is just useless review,' or 'Let's get on with it already!'

"After getting an account on a new system, I will spend as many hours as possible on that system – twenty or twenty-four hours at a time on one account, if the system is something that I haven't seen before, or if it has programs or text on it that interest me. I need to learn as much as I possibly can: not only everything about the computer itself, but everything about the data, too. Computers are convenient, and they interest me to begin with, but once I am on your system, I'll be quite content to learn about your company's management structure – if that's all there is available."

Students are bright, and they are bored. They are smart enough to know they have a lot to learn, and what interests them most is what they can find out next. As the name implies, this is a stage from which one can only graduate by finding out *how* to graduate.

For me, and most of my friends, the excitement comes in learning something I did not know a moment before. I love to know more than I did a few minutes ago, as I think most people do.

Imagine yourself in a huge library. As far as you can see, information that interests you is lying about. When you are on a system, it feels as if you are following the stacks, until you come to something you don't know and would like to learn. You spend several hours learning it. There is a possibility that you will not understand it, but that is not a problem – in fact, when you come back to it in a few days and *do* understand it, you feel as if you have learned that much more.

By the end of a typical day, a Student may have visited several computer systems, whose total hardware value could be in the tens of millions of dollars, and he may feel that he has learned twice as much in one day as he has during the entire school year.

Hacking is basically a solitary pastime, especially for Students, who like working on their own. But hackers are no more or less anti-social than the rest of the world and, like anyone else, they enjoy "bumping into" acquaintances. During a trip around his various accounts, a Student may, for instance, run into a friend from Florida while exploring a DEC-20 in New York. The "meeting" would look something like the following exchange.

> Other Hacker: Scan? Is that you?
> Student: Who's this?
> Other Hacker: This is Sentinel from Florida.
> Student: Hi. How did you find me?
> Other Hacker: You have NAME set to HACKER_SCAN.
> I thought it sounded like you. I have an operator account for an HP-3000. Want it?
> Student: I forgot that I set my name. Operator account? Sure.
> Other Hacker: It's that 3000 we had a few months ago. The account is OPERATOR.SYS LOVE.
> Student: Thanks. Let's see ... I can give you a new Cyber account I have:705-555-3242 4334,SECRET. You know how to use a Cyber, right?
> Other Hacker: I won't even answer that one. Got to go ... bye.
> Student: Bye. See you around.

Here's what happened during this conversation: The Sentinel (who lives in Florida) and Scan were both on the same computer. The Sentinel had checked out other users by running a program that listed who was currently on the system, and he had noticed the user name HACKER_SCAN. Thinking he might know this person, The Sentinel risked "talking" to him. Once they had established who they were, The Sentinel offered Scan access to a very powerful operator's account on an HP-3000 computer. This offer was accepted, and Scan returned the favor by giving away his new account on a Cyber computer.

If you discover a Student on your system, consider yourself lucky in two aspects: lucky that he's a Student and not a destructive hacker, and lucky that you found him at all. A Student would never intentionally damage a system, because there's no reason why he should and there are many good reasons why he shouldn't. He spent as much as twenty to forty hours just to get access to the system, and he wants to remain undiscovered, if at all possible, so he can keep using the computer. He also wants to stay out of any and all trouble. He spends long hours in cracking a system, so he respects the work of the system's programmers and wants to avoid giving them extra work. Besides, he knows that he may someday want to apply for a job with your company or perhaps request an account as a favor (it's very nice to get official use of a computer system).

However, assuming the Student has enough time, he will, out of curiosity, sooner or later examine every file on your system, and for some companies this prospect can be dangerous in its own right. I have never known a Student to abuse information he found, but then if you have the log-on procedures to your high-security computer stored as a file on your low-security computer, the potential for abuse – if not by the Student, then by someone less "ethical" – certainly does exist.

And one final note: A Student often roams undiscovered on your system until he walks in looking for a job. When you see his resumé, you will find that he's had three years' experience on the same computer you have, doing the same type of programming you need done. Strange, but somehow Students seem to know just the person you want to hire ... and when.

The Tourist   Unlike the Student, the Tourist is out for nothing more than an adventure or the challenge of solving a puzzle. Quite often he obtains an account, simply looks around for a few minutes, and leaves, never to return again. Why would someone spend so much time doing something without reward? For the Tourist, hacking is a form of mental game, like a crossword puzzle. His reward is the "thrill of victory" he feels after succeeding in his quest. This is how a Tourist once described his hacking to me.

"You have to decide in advance what system you are going to get into. It's always best if you just pull a name of a large company or corporation out of the phone book at random; that way, you can succeed on two levels. When you discover how to call into a computer you weren't quite sure existed the day before, that's a small victory in itself. Then, after you have decided to try getting into the computer, you start to draw up a game plan. In many cases, you can succeed simply by calling the company and convincing some secretary to give you an account but, in most cases, you simply get a user name from the company and get to work on hacking the password.

"It's usually very simple to tell what kind of password will most likely be in heavy use. In almost every case, at least two to three percent of the passwords on a given system will be first names – possibly as many as twenty percent. Quite often ten or twelve percent of the passwords will be single character. After you have a user name, you can start hacking. . . .

"It's got to be done a hundred percent by hand, because it isn't even worth it to set up your computer to try a hundred thousand different passwords. The main problems with using the computer [to search for valid passwords] are that it isn't nearly as much fun if you do succeed, and the computer has no 'feel' for trying passwords in different situations. Secondary problems include the fact that it gets hard to trust a computer if it reports NO SUCCESS after ten or fifteen hours.

"Anyway, after you've got your account name and password, you just log on to make sure that the computer is nothing special . . . like a top-secret military computer or an FBI training computer. If it isn't, then you write all the information down and save it for possible later use. If you do ever use the account again, it will most likely be to trade information with other hackers. Getting in with a traded name and password isn't nearly as gratifying as getting in yourself, but it's still fun to look at what other people are doing."

You can see that the Tourist is a person who needs a good puzzle from time to time. I think there are two characteristics that a hacker needs in order to be a Tourist. First, he needs to be someone who feels that he has to test himself. Second, I think he needs a very mathematical mind because he is always figuring the odds: "Suppose I spend thirty hours on this system. With the information I now have, will cracking the system be worth the time?" "How likely is it that I'll get in with this or that method?"

Every now and then a Student or a Crasher (whom I'll describe next) will contact a Tourist and ask him to get a password to a particular system. When the Tourist decides to try such jobs, he succeeds probably eight or nine times out of ten — but it may take him as long as a year. A Tourist is a fairly safe type of hacker, because he has no interest in being destructive. There is a fairly strong possibility, however, that the Tourist will trade the password to your system off to a more destructive friend at some point, because using the system is not as important to him as it is to a Student. Getting in is the name of his game.

The Crasher You won't know you have a Crasher on your system until it's too late: until you hear from an irate user that three weeks' work has been destroyed and you find the words THE MAD CRASHER STRIKES filling all two and a half billion characters of your disk space.

The Crasher seems to operate with little or no logical purpose. He is a troublemaker, motivated by the same elusive goals as a vandal. If it weren't for computers, he could just as easily be spray-painting his name on the side of a building, or perhaps even setting the building on fire. As far as I can tell, a Crasher's only purpose is to make himself as visible as possible among his peers and his victims. To attain this lofty goal, he works to cause you as much trouble as he possibly can. And to make sure you know who did it, he chooses a name, such as Crasher One, that leaves no doubt in your mind.

I remember one Crasher who was bragging (a common activity) about how he crashed one particular system. He was proud of this one, because he had obtained the system operator's password — something that's genuinely worth bragging about. After getting the password, he waited a few days until the company was ready to back up the system according to a schedule he had found. (Backing up is the process of transferring information from the system onto tape to ensure against accidental – or deliberate – loss. Most systems make it easy for a hacker or anyone else to check on the last backup; sometimes, each file has the last backup date on it.)

The Crasher waited until the time was right for his purposes. Just before the backup procedure started, when his "strike" would damage the most data and thus have the greatest impact on everyone concerned, he proceeded to erase all the files – no problem, if you have succeeded in hacking the system operator's password. I remember afterward he said something like, "I thought they would only be down a few hours and maybe lose a few days' work. But it's been over two weeks now and they are still down." He was very happy about that particular result.

At the least destructive end of the Crasher spectrum, a system crash can simply consist of removing one user's electronic mail, or of removing a single account so that its owner cannot log on until an operator reactivates the account. On the other hand, a Crasher's activity can, and has, escalated as far as erasure of all programs and data on the system, and to actual physical attacks on the computer. In most cases, you can expect a Crasher's tampering to result in several important files, accounts, or both, going dead.

In general, before he makes his move, the Crasher will hole up and spend a few hours reconnoitering the target system on Sunday night. At this time, he will find out as much as he can about how the system is run, and he will use what he learns to decide how he's going to crash the system for the greatest possible effect. This is when you have the best chance of spotting and stopping him, because this is the time he is finding out how *not* to get caught. After his reconnaissance, when he knows what he will do – and when – the Crasher will log off and bide his time, waiting for the Big Moment.

Depending on how the system is run, he may wait for several days. Sometimes, for example, he'll wait until the following Friday night, because he thinks that no qualified personnel will be available until Monday to take care of the problems he causes: All the people who want to use the computer from a terminal over the weekend will have to wait, and he will have intensified the losses inflicted on his victims' time, efforts, and patience.

For the most part, Crashers usually don't rate very high in the estimation of other hackers. This is because Crashers do three things that most hackers don't like:

■ *They give all hackers a bad name.*

■ *They close down accounts that other hackers spend much time and effort to get.*

■ *They often attempt to crash bulletin-board systems – the places that most hackers use to communicate.*

To sum it all up: They are not very nice guys.

The Thief   The Thief is the rarest type of hacker. In fact, by my own and most other hackers' definitions, the Thief is not a hacker at all: He is a criminal. Although he is much more professional than any other hacker, the Thief's motives are perhaps the easiest to explain: He wants to profit at your expense. In a majority of cases, there is no direct financial gain involved; the profit usually takes the form of data stolen from a competing company.

There is a fair chance that a Thief will include a bribed or blackmailed employee, a wiretap system, or some similar "standard" spying techniques in his plan. Much more often, though, a Thief is part of the company that is being robbed. He is seldom discovered, and simply continues to drain away tens of thousands of dollars worth of information. The Thief's victim, meanwhile, has no idea that anything of the sort is going on.

Recent figures, cited in the Institute of Electrical and Electronic Engineers' journal *Spectrum* ("Can Computer Crime Be Stopped?" May 1984), estimate that thieves collectively take as much as three billion dollars from industry every year. While some authorities feel that as many as five or ten percent of these thieves are caught, they quite often get off with little or no punishment because, as the saying goes, "all they did was push buttons."

The law is changing rapidly in the area of high-tech theft, but very few people in the criminal-justice system yet have a real understanding of the technological details of computer crime. And that is one reason why these thieves are rarely prosecuted. One example cited in the *Spectrum* article was that of a district attorney who failed to prosecute the thief of a computer program estimated to be worth over a million dollars. His reason for failing to prosecute was: "Why go to court over $70 worth of punch cards?"

Most computer systems won't ever be bothered by a Thief, but those that are will suffer significant losses – losses that can be particularly troublesome because they are difficult to measure.

Because I feel that this subject is not computer hacking, but computer crime, I don't consider myself qualified to tell you how to secure your system from a Thief. Clearly, if you have Thief-tempting information or software on what you hope is a secure system, you would be wise to try and eliminate the possibility that a Thief will find his way into your files. If so, you may want to seek out other sources of information or turn to well-qualified consultants for advice. Common sense and the precautions suggested in this book should be enough to protect most current computer systems from most current computer hackers. If you are in any doubt about your system, however, my best suggestion would be to hire a professional security consultant with good references.

How much trouble will a hacker go to, if he wants to get onto your computer? How much time and effort will he dedicate to breaking your system's security? The answers depend on several factors, especially the type of hacker and the nature of your system.

TO WHAT EXTENT A HACKER HACKS

The first – and least – level of effort that you will encounter is both the most common and the safest from your point of view. Most hackers are just looking for an open door so, at this level, the hacker is nosing around, but has no particular reason to get onto your particular system. He has simply found or been given the system's phone number or network address and wants to check out your front-line security. He will spend a few minutes with your system, testing for a few very basic security flaws – for example, commonly used account names, such as DEMO, TEST, GAMES, the name of the company, or a few of his own

The First Level

tried-and-true favorites. If he doesn't get into your computer, he will, at least fifty to sixty percent of the time, just move on to some other company's computer system.

Although this first level of hacking demands little effort and less determination, you would be quite surprised at how successful hackers could be if they never tried anything more. I remember one system that had a DEMO account with no password. All anyone had to do was call the computer and type DEMO. After I had been on the system awhile, I was contacted by the system operators, who were certain that I must have had contacts inside the company. Again and again they asked me, "How did you know about this account?" Again and again I replied, "I just guessed." It's human nature, I suppose: System programmers hate to admit that they left gaping holes in the system's security, and system operators are loath to admit that they left such breaches unrepaired.

The Second Level   The second level of effort is usually expended by a hacker who happens to like your computer system. Most hackers find themselves liking one particular computer or operating system more than any other, and to get onto one of these systems, they are willing to expend a little extra effort. If your system happens to be a hacker's favorite, you can expect him to go beyond level one to test a few weaknesses that he knows are unique to your system. Some versions of the Primos operating system, for example, have built-in accounts that the system "defaults" to, unless told otherwise, and that are well known to hackers, who use them to gain access to the system. Some adaptations of UNIX, another major operating system, sometimes have what hackers call a "rapid-fire" loophole, which fools the operating system by having it carry out a "high-level" command, when only a "low-level" one has been approved. If such level-two attempts don't succeed, the hacker might then get serious and move up to level three, if he hasn't had an account on his favorite system in awhile.

Hackers working on level two, however, usually don't like machines that are on networks, because a network machine tends to receive more than its share of hacking, and so its security weaknesses are generally exposed by hackers and fixed by operators early in the system's life. If a hacker is trying to get an account on a computer that is part of a public network, he often just goes directly to level three.

Level three is where the hacker really starts spending time on your system. It may be that he has some inside information that will make his job easier, or it simply may be that he specifically wants access to your computer (possibly because of your company name or because of the size or type of your computer). *The Third Level*

At this point a hacker may start actually hacking. He may use a database hack (described in the next chapter), which electronically tries out a "library" of commonly used passwords, but more likely, he will stick to making somewhere between forty and seventy educated guesses at a viable password. The hacker on level three often ends up succeeding without moving on to level four. If he has tried and failed, he will move on about seventy-five to eighty-five percent of the time.

Level four is usually left to the Tourists, who are notorious for going to extreme efforts to attain their goals. While some Tourists give up after failing at levels one, two, and three, others feel that they must get into your system or "lose the game," so they move on to the more advanced techniques of level four. They may resort to researching your system users, or to visiting your computer room to look over shoulders or to read scribbled notes left near terminals. Or, they may set up a computer to try every possible password – if that is what's required. *The Fourth Level*

A hacker working at level four succeeds in getting into a system about ninety percent of the time. It is very possible, however, that the system operators will be aware of him and throw him off the system once he gets in, and for two reasons: First, the system is fairly secure and the system operators may well be alert enough to find him and, second, the hacker himself probably created quite a bit of detectable evidence while he was operating at or building up to level four.

Level five consists of measures taken only by a Thief, unless you have a *very* determined Tourist or Crasher on your hands. A hacker operating at this level may plant bugs, bribe or blackmail employees, or pose as a computer technician. More likely, though, he will be an employee *The Fifth Level* of the company that owns the computer. If you catch a hacker using level-five techniques, take a look at the trail he left in your system. If the hacker started out at level five, then he is very likely a Thief, because other hackers will move up through the lower levels. In most cases, a hacker on level five hopes your system will directly or indirectly provide a material gain for him, so he is willing to invest much time, effort, even money, in staying out of trouble. He is also, for these reasons, very difficult to find and catch.

CHAPTER FIVE

How a Hacker Hacks

Not long before I became a member of the Inner Circle, I was exploring computers on my own when I happened upon a very low-security password to a mainframe computer used by an East Coast university. Designed primarily for demonstrations, this account didn't allow users to do anything very interesting (at least as far as I was concerned). None of the computer's more powerful programs could be accessed by this account, and the storage space allotted to the account was very limited. This demonstration account was good for starters, but I really wanted a better account on that system – one that did not restrict my explorations as much as this one did. And to get that better account, I needed leverage; I found it in the operating system.

This system, like many mainframes at the time, had one very interesting feature: If a person were to use a modem to call into his or her account, then hang up *without logging off,* the first person to phone in on the same line in the next ten minutes would automatically be connected to the open account. What was actually happening here was a phone-based version of a situation in which someone walks away from a terminal for a few minutes without logging off: Anyone who might wander by could sit down and start using the open account, and the computer would have no way of knowing whether the activity on the account was coming from the authorized user or an intruder.

To me, this feature meant that I could, in theory, use someone else's account – possibly a much higher-level account than mine. But most people do log off, so my chances of calling into an open account really were not very good. Then too, even if I did manage to call into someone's account, I would have no way of learning the password, so I could use the account only once. Not good enough.

There was another way, though. A way that would make this feature of the system work for me: I could call and hang up on my own account, my low-level account. That would leave the account open for the next caller. Now, if that next caller did not know my account was open and waiting – if that next caller tried to log onto the system – he or she would very naturally enter both an account name *and* a password. If I could then somehow read what the caller typed, I would be able to use that person's account. And I could keep trying the same thing (assuming I wasn't detected by the system operator) until I got the type of high-level account I was after. Or, at the very least, I should be able to use one of the new account/password combinations that I "eavesdropped" on to better my position somehow on the system.

Eventually, I did end up with a high-level position on that system, and I did it by writing a program, known to hackers as a decoy, that pretended to be the operating system. When I left my original, low-level account open, I also left this program running. When the next call came into the system on my "open" phone line, my decoy program displayed for the caller all of the "hello, please log on" messages that the operating system itself would normally display. The difference was, my program stored the caller's account and password information in a special file I had set up for myself in the host system. Once the caller had entered the information I wanted, I had the decoy program display a message along the lines of "sorry, try again," and turn control over to the real operating system so the caller's next attempt to log on would be successful – and no one was any the wiser.

One of the great appeals of hacking is the practical way in which it builds on itself. New skills become old skills, but not before they've provided a hacker with the foundation for a bigger and better "bag of tricks" and a more sophisticated way of hacking.

While the word *hacking* itself implies that a person spends time chopping away at something, about the only thing that a high-level hacker hacks at in this sense (using techniques I'll explain shortly) is a password. Once a hacker has an account and password that allow him access to a computer, his hacking becomes the type of planned and deliberately executed activity that I tried to illustrate in the preceding story. At this point, hacking is hands-on learning and testing, an exciting enterprise that depends on experience, skill, and a knowledge of computers and computer operating systems. Now, the hacker is trying to find his way to the top of the system, undetected. His goal: the rights and privileges of the sysop himself and, with them, the freedom to explore the computer and its files at will.

There are many techniques a hacker uses to try and attain this ultimate goal. A few of them are based on educated guesses, but most of a hacker's approaches are based on experiments – experiments that can range from trial-and-error "if at first you don't succeed" attempts to hack a password up to elaborate, controlled programs designed to test, trick, or maneuver around the operating system, the system operator, or both.

A hacker may learn how to hack from other hackers or from hands-on experience, but when he begins to spend hour after hour playing with large computer systems and trying to gain access to them, he very soon learns all the tricks that make life easier for him. This chapter will tell you about the various tricks and techniques in the hacker's "toolkit," but it's important to realize that this toolkit goes hand-in-glove with the hacker's approach to hacking. Ultimately, the way a hacker thinks is what distinguishes one hacker from another. Just as a carpenter and a cabinetmaker can use many of the same tools, but do vastly different things with them, so can a Student and a Tourist, or a Tourist and a Crasher. Their approaches are different, their goals are different, and most importantly, their "products" are different, with different implications for your system's security.

A HACKER'S
APPROACH

Normally, two steps are involved in the basic methods hackers use to gain unauthorized access to computers: First the hacker obtains an account. That's the easy part—sometimes it's as easy as calling and asking for one (posing as a university student, perhaps); more usually, it means getting account names from bulletin boards, company phone lists, or trash bins...maybe using a friend's or relative's account on THE SOURCE. There are many ways, because account names are not secret—the computer calls the user by this name or number, and users often refer to other users by their accounts. It is the *password* that is a secret. Therefore, a hacker's second step involves ways of faking or discovering passwords. This is one of the areas in which lax security makes the hacker's job easier than it need be: Well-chosen passwords that are easy to remember, but difficult for a hacker to guess (yes, there are such things), and educated users who keep secret passwords secret are a very effective defense at this level of security.

GENERAL
METHODS

As mentioned, hackers have a whole toolkit that they use to obtain passwords and gain control of accounts. Three of a hacker's most important resources, however, are actually general, rather than specific, methods of unlocking computers. These methods involve thinking about "how to hack systems." They are: thinking like a user, conducting independent "research," and using a system's defaults, which are its built-in assumptions about user needs.

*Thinking Like
A User*

Hacking is a game of wits, and the people who are drawn to it are the same type of people who like to play chess or mental games with unseen opponents. Part of the "psychology" of hacking involves cultivating a skill for stepping into the shoes of the person who operates or uses a computer system that a hacker seeks to penetrate.

The best hackers know that it is important to think like a user. They constantly say to themselves, "What would I do if *I* were this user?" If they are good at this kind of parallel thinking, they quite often have very accurate insights into the word a user decides on as a password. A user, remember, is anyone in a company or a university who needs to use a computer to perform *tasks:* an executive who uses

76

a spreadsheet program; a secretary who uses a word processor; a scientist, engineer, or scholar who uses the computer to perform research calculations. And the characteristic all these people share is not that they are fascinated by or know a lot about computers, but that they want to get a job done. Often, they know very little about aspects of the system that are not directly related to their needs.

Because computer users think of computers as tools, they are often quite easy for a hacker to second-guess. For example, if they don't know or understand the significance of a password, they may consider this very basic element of computer security as a simple nuisance. And, in that case, they are quite inclined to choose a password that is simple, easy to remember – and easy for a hacker to guess. On the other hand, maybe they really can't believe that anyone would try to look *inside the computer* at MegaCar's design memos or the results of their latest research project, even though they would be very careful of the same information once it had been printed out on paper.

Uneducated users with attitudes like these represent a serious concern for security-minded system owners and operators. If someone were to attempt to talk to them through the system, they would have no way of telling a hacker from a system operator. From both hearsay and experience, I can verify that many users never suspect that the person asking for their password is a sixteen-year-old hacker living two thousand miles away.

In a few cases, I have noticed that the need for management to make computing cost-effective also seems to come into the picture. After spending $30 million on a computer system that is not being used to its full potential, management will often give accounts to people who have little desire or use for them. These users can end up with several accounts on various company computers and, in such cases, the users almost always use the same password for each account. Here again, they are also likely to make it an easily remembered password, and on top of that, since they don't often use the system, they rarely note unusual (hacker) activity on their accounts.

Sometimes, however, it is not enough to pretend to be a user and to try thinking like one. Sometimes a hacker has to take steps to find out how

Research

the users of certain computers actually think and what they actually know. Often, this kind of research extends beyond the limits of what a hacker can discover with only a computer and modem.

I once became involved in a "research" project when several hackers were having trouble getting access to an IBM-370 — a state-of-the-art mainframe. Ordinarily, hardware is less important than software, and software is not as important as the procedures used to access and run the computer. In this case, however, the computer was sealed tight at all levels. None of the usual or unusual tricks of the trade succeeded in turning up a viable password.

The frustrated hackers sent out a message to The Cracker on a private bulletin-board system they had been directed to by a member of the Inner Circle. I answered, but I could do very little to help them technically. This system had tight security, savvy system operators who were unsympathetic to hackers, and sophisticated users. Then I had an idea: Just because a computer is tightly secured doesn't mean that the company throws unauthorized visitors out of the lobby.

One of the hackers lived near the company, so I suggested that he write and print a one-page questionnaire on a letter-quality printer. He was to stand in the lobby and hand out about 150 copies to employees as they entered and left the building. He was to look and act student-like, and represent the questionnaire as a class project. The form asked the employee to answer some questions: name, address, job description, title, whether or not the respondent used a computer at work and so on, along the same lines. It also requested the employees to leave the form in a certain place for collection.

The strategy worked and, after the papers were collected, all the resourceful hackers needed to do was to try different bits of information as passwords. In that particular case, the first names of the employees worked but, if not, the hackers could have tried the names of wives, pets, cars, whatever — there were plenty of leads on those completed questionnaires.

Of course, if the hacker had been asked to leave the company building, he could also have left the questionnaires on the windshields of the cars in the parking lot. Or he could have copied down some of the license-plate numbers and then obtained the employees' home addresses (from the Department of Motor Vehicles – possibly at a cost of two dollars), so he could visit them personally, pretending it was a door-to-door survey.

As this example illustrates, it happens that seemingly irrelevant scraps of information (the name of a user's pet dog, for example) can often come in handy for the hacker. And good hackers try to collect and remember everything they come across – information from questionnaires, "chance" encounters with employees, conversations with sympathetic system operators, the contents of electronic-mail files, or anything they might learn about the company whose computer they are trying to crack. If there's a moral to this story, it's a very simple one: Educate your system's users.

The most powerful computers have the most complicated operating systems. And a powerful, complicated operating system has many more options than any but the most fanatically devoted user would ever be interested in using. For example, when a system operator is given the task of creating a new account for a new user, there may be several hundred different account "attributes" to set. These attributes include such things as level of security, account name or number, account password, and whether or not the user has the power to erase other users' files.

Defaults

Because of the large number of potential attributes that can be assigned to a given account, every complicated operating system has many *defaults* that automatically select options instead of requiring someone to specify them. A default is any option that gets "assigned" because it is the most likely choice. For example, since very few users have the power to erase other people's files, the attribute that decides whether a user has this power may automatically *default* to "no" if the operator does not specifically assign "yes."

In some cases, default accounts, rather than just options, are present on a system to perform housekeeping functions, such as taking care of backup files or watching over help files; in others, default passwords are used. In some of the less helpful, but still very popular, defaults, last names are used as accounts or birthdates are used as passwords. Defaults make life easier for system operators, because the operators can simply write a program that says "last name = account name, birthdate = password," and so on, and then the program will go through a user's file and assign the correct default settings quickly and automatically.

Hackers love defaults. They make life easier for hackers, too. Defaults seem to be a hacker-friendly feature that will be with the world as long as computers need complicated operating systems – and that means they will be with us for the foreseeable future.

Hackers could probably spend the rest of their lives finding out about and using all the various default values, simply because they are there, and no one ever seems to want to change them. Certain versions of one operating system gained a reputation in the hacking community in terms of defaults. These were versions of Primos, now a very secure operating system that is run on Prime computers. (If you are not familiar with these machines, Prime computers are the ones used by THE SOURCE, a popular information utility that more than fifty thousand owners of personal computers use via their modems to find out about the stock market, make airline reservations, research the utility's information data bases, and exchange information with other subscribers.)

The major security problem with these versions of Primos is that they had certain default accounts that existed when the system was first installed – accounts that were not meant to be used, and that had no passwords. These accounts existed primarily as maintenance accounts for the system – various programs could be set up to run "under" these accounts.

SPECIFIC METHODS

Thinking like a user, research, and defaults are all-purpose elements of a hacker's toolkit, but most of the methods used by hackers involve much more specific techniques. Through the process of trial and error, and from their own knowledge of telecommunications networks and operating systems, hackers have developed a number of approaches to hacking passwords, obtaining new accounts, and working inside the system. The rest of the descriptions in this chapter are of just such specific tools.

The basic form of the hack-hack method is the technique non-hackers most commonly associate with hacking. It is also a technique that is seldom used by anyone but the rawest Novices. A hacker using a "pure" version of the hack-hack method would do the following: First, he would obtain at least one account name; more likely he would get five to ten. Then, he would program a personal computer to: (1) phone the remote computer, (2) transmit the account names he had obtained, and (3) try different passwords on each account name. These password attempts would be generated by the hacker's program and could be either random strings of characters or sequential attempts, such as AAAAAA, AAAAAB, AAAAAC, AAAAAD, and so on.

Hack-Hack

On the surface, the hack-hack method sounds simple and logical, but if you think about it, there is almost no way, other than sheer accident, that a hacker could be very successful using this method with currently available computer technology. In fact, rumors floating around the hacker underground claim that the only people who use this method work for government task forces (in either investigative or intelligence agencies); they are the only people who have the giant, high-speed supercomputers that can do such a task successfully.

Even if a hacker could program his computer to try a new password, say, once every ten seconds (very unlikely, because the remote computer will probably take longer than that to respond to each attempt), and even if he limited the words to four upper- or lowercase letters of the alphabet, it could easily take the hacker almost two months of twenty-four-hour hacking to go through every possible combination. In addition, he would need to try these passwords on at least three or four accounts.

But this situation, really, is the best of all possible worlds. In most cases, the hacker would face even more problems: He could only try (on average) once every fifteen or twenty seconds. He would have to assume that the passwords were at least six characters long. He might need to use *both* upper- and lowercase letters. In many cases, spaces or other non-alphabetic characters might very well be used.

(Just for fun, you can figure out what kind of time would be involved here. Attempting one six-character combination of upper- and lowercase letters every twenty seconds, the hacker would take more than twelve-and-a-half thousand years to go through every possible combination. Obviously, he would get lucky at some point but, even so, that hacker could be at it a *long* time.)

If, after all that work, the hacker should become very lucky and get a valid password with the hack-hack method, the system operators would be ready and waiting for him: There wouldn't be any way they could *not* notice such constant hacking.

A sysop watching an account while a hack-hack attack was under way would see that not only was the user making repeated attempts to enter a password, but that the passwords differed according to a set pattern—AAA, AAB, AAC, for example. Even a system operator who did not have to be particularly careful about security would be very likely to spot such a systematic attempt to guess a password.

Variations
On a Theme

There are, however, a few more sensible versions of the hack-hack method. The first of these, the short hack, is very straightforward testing of five to fifteen or thirty accounts. This method assumes that one of these accounts will have a *single-character* password, so it will try each account either twenty-six times (once for each letter of the alphabet) or fifty-two times (if both upper- and lowercase are needed). A hacker might do this testing manually, but since it is the type of tedious but systematic task that computers can do so well, it is more likely that the hacker will write a simple program to try all these variations and notify him when one of the variations is successful.

This method has many problems of its own, but when it's successful, the hacker can often be on the system the day after he starts. Single-character passwords are very convenient for users to remember. And no hacker is going to argue with results.

A second variation of the hack-hack method tackles the problem from the other side. It is called the reverse hack, and instead of trying many possible passwords on one account, it takes two or three very common passwords and tests them on anywhere from twenty to two hundred accounts. For example, the word *password*, obvious as it seems, is very often used by naive users. If a hacker had a list of twenty account names, he could use the reverse hack by programming his computer to call the remote system and try the word *password* as a password on each of the account names. The reverse hack quite often bypasses some system security because, on many systems, the operator doesn't get notified of two or three unsuccessful log-on attempts on one account – the computer only notifies him about many unsuccessful attempts on one account.

From my experience, it seems most people don't pay much attention to choosing their "secret" passwords. By browsing and experimenting, I've found that the three most common password choices are *secret, love,* and *sex . . .* though not necessarily in that order.

Both the hack-hack and reverse-hack methods rely heavily on chance, so it is very hard to predict whether these methods will succeed in ten minutes or ten hours. A third variation, however, is perhaps the most often successful as far as these methods go. It is known as the database hack. The hacker who uses this method tries ten to twenty accounts, and he tries passwords to these from a data base, or "library," of anywhere from twenty to five hundred commonly used passwords. The data base contains words that the hacker knows to be common passwords. A typical file would contain such entries as: Love, Sex, Secret, Demo, Games, Test, Account, Intro, Password, Alpha, Hello, Kill, Beta, Dollar, Dead, System, Computer, Work, Yes, No, Please, Ok, Okay, God *(popular with system operators),* Superuser *(another good one for sysops),* Aid, Help, the name of the company, formatted in various ways, for example, MegaCar, Mcar, Megcar, Mega, MC, Car, the letters A through Z, two to four hundred first names, possibly ten or twenty names of pop musical groups, possibly five to ten names of automobiles, the digits 0 through 9.

While it is quite often successful, the database hack is normally used only on systems where the system operator is either known to be sympathetic to hackers or just doesn't care, because this is another method that, with its repeated attempts on the system, will probably have the system operator waiting once the hacker gets in.

The Decoy

The three hack-hack variations are very simple and are used mostly by novice hackers. Higher-level hackers prefer to use their wits, instead of a brute-force assault. One of the more sophisticated hacking tools is known as the decoy, and it comes in three versions.

The first version of this trick is the one I described at the beginning of this chapter, and it requires that the hacker have an account on the system in question. As in my case, the hacker has a low-security account, and he tries this method to get a higher-security account. He will first use his low-security account to write a program that will emulate the log-on procedures of the system in question. This program will do the following:

≡ *Clear the terminal screen and place text on it that makes everything look as if the system is in charge.*

≡ *Prompt for, and allow the user to enter, both an account name and a password.*

≡ *Save that information in a place the hacker can access.*

≡ *Tell the user the account/password entries are not acceptable.*

≡ *Turn control of the terminal back over to the system.*

The user will now assume that the account name or password was mistyped and will try again...this time (since the real operating system is in control) with more success. You can see a diagram of the way these steps are accomplished on the following page.

After writing this program, the hacker can either set it running from afar, as I did, or, if he has access to the building, he can go to various terminals and run his program on each one individually. Regardless, when the people try to log on to their accounts, the hacker's program will record the users' accounts and passwords. In many cases the hacker may have his program tell the user that the system is down for five minutes, rather than have it tell him to try again. In any case, the user will have to log on again.

The decoy is potentially even more useful to a hacker if he has a little bit of help from the phone company, and a handy service known as call forwarding.

Many people use call forwarding by special arrangement with the phone company. When a customer requests call forwarding, the phone company uses its computers to forward all the customer's incoming calls to another number. Let's say, for example, that you want

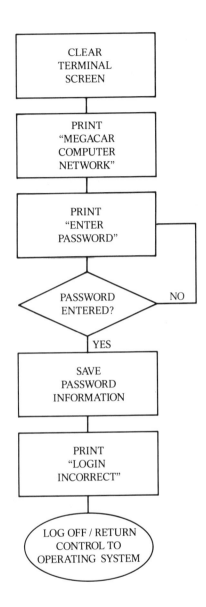

calls that come to your office phone to be forwarded to your home phone: A call from you to the phone company, some special settings in the phone company's computer, and all calls to your office will ring at your home instead.

Law-abiding citizens can simply request call forwarding; hackers have to be less direct, since they are forwarding someone else's number, not their own. Still, this obstacle is usually not a problem, since many hackers also happen to work for the telephone company. In one case, I helped a group of hackers use call forwarding to gain access to a Prime computer in their vicinity. This system was hooked up to one of the phone company's more advanced switching systems, so it was a simple matter to have a contact within the phone company set call forwarding on the phone line going into the system in question. After my contact set call forwarding on our target's number, I told the hacker how to go to the building housing the computer and set call forwarding to one of the group's phone numbers. There, they had a personal computer waiting with a decoy program set up to mimic the real system. This decoy allowed a caller to enter an account and password, then it displayed an appropriate "log-on unsuccessful" message and hung up on the caller. Even though it emulated the real system for only a matter of seconds, the decoy program kept the forwarded line open for five minutes after terminating the user's call. This was because we expected the user to call back and try to log on again. To avoid suspicion, we wanted the second attempt to be successful. By keeping "our" line open, we could ensure that the user's next call would go through on a "real" line to the real computer.

There are a few other versions of the decoy trick that hackers use, too. One is very similar to the last I described. The hacker must write essentially the same program, to display the text that simulates the target computer's log-on sequence. He also must have some type of account on the computer. In addition, the computer system in question must have some form of *chat, send,* or *talk* program that enables the user of one account to interact with the user of another.

To put this version to work, the hacker must first establish contact with the person using the account for which he wants the password. The hacker will then activate his decoy program, which will send text to the remote user. The text will inform the user of a "fatal error" (a bit of computer jargon that simply means "you messed up," even though it often strikes terror into the heart of a naive user), and then the decoy program will simulate the log-on sequence. The user is still logged on, still doing whatever he or she was doing. But suddenly, text appears on the screen requesting another log-on attempt, after which the hacker allows the user back onto the system.

This trick is infamous for fooling subscribers of THE SOURCE and CompuServe (another commercial information utility.) In fact, every time you enter a program to talk with other users on Compu-Serve, you see the message: WARNING: NEVER ENTER YOUR PASS-WORD WHILE IN CB OR TALK. This precaution is a good idea for any system that allows users to interact.

Another version of this technique differs a great deal from the other two in that this procedure needs much more help from a user. Version three is usually only effective when the hacker is trying to get an account from a service computer, such as the ones used by Dow Jones, THE SOURCE, CompuServe, DIALOG, or any of the other timeshare-oriented computers serving a large number of people. This trick goes something like this:

The hacker contacts a person who uses the computer he wants access to – perhaps he knows the person, or perhaps he might buy a mailing list from the computer-owning company itself. In his contact (either a letter or a phone call), the hacker says that a new, local dial-up service is available that will be cheaper and faster to use, and he lists the phone number to call. The hacker has a personal computer set up at the phone number to emulate the system the user expects to see. Once the user calls the number with his own terminal and enters his account and password, the hacker's program tells the user that the dial-up service is not available at this time, but that he will receive a no-tice from the company once it is.

Computer memory is roughly comparable to, say, the cells in a bee-hive. Altogether, these "cells" can hold a great deal of information. Each cell, however, is also an independent unit, with its own location (*address* in computer terminology) and its own storage capacity.

Using Computer Memory

Hackers sometimes find that a particular operating system will allow them to do things directly to memory that they otherwise could not do, and many hackers try, sooner or later, to gain access to inde-pendent memory locations in the target computer. Obviously, if you have the power to change what is stored in the target computer's memory, you have the power to command that computer to do all sorts of things. This method of hacking tries to bypass the operating system altogether, and requires knowledge of mainframe computer programming, since such programming tools are what you need if you want to change the contents of the computer's memory. One common way hackers use this technique is in accessing the text buffers (the place in the target computer's memory where incoming keystrokes are collected) to find out what a user entered as a password. Another possibility in some systems is changing a cell in memory so that you can erase a file you do not have authorization to erase – an important point, since erasing files is sometimes necessary to *prevent* damage.

Quite often, hackers use BASIC programs to manipulate memory, but any one of several other computer languages could also be used; BASIC, because it is so common, is simply the language most likely to be "understood" by a target computer. If you know BASIC programming, you know that most versions of BASIC use two commands to access independent memory locations: PEEK to read the contents, and POKE to change what's there. You use a PEEK command to find out exactly what information is stored at a specific location in your target computer's memory. Then, if you want, you can use a POKE command to change the contents of that location, and thus change the way the target computer operates.

One Inner Circle member used a BASIC program of this sort to PEEK at passwords stored in the memory of a computer located in the research-and-development department of a major corporation. First, the hacker created a file named Top Secret, which was placed in a "common area" that all accounts would access and was certain to attract the curiosity of users, who would want to run the program just to find out what it did. In this case, whenever curious users ran the file, they saw an innocuous message: I SAID THIS WAS TOP SECRET!! Little did they know that running the file did a lot more than type a silly message onto the screen. (Technically, this kind of file is another kind of hacker's trick, known as a Trojan horse, which is explained in detail later. In this case, however, it serves as an interesting example of the way in which a hacker can manipulate computer memory.)

Because the hacker had done some previous exploring with the POKE and PEEK commands, he had been able to find the memory location where his own password was kept while he was logged on. He figured he could write a program including a routine that used the PEEK command to look at these memory locations, and when other people ran his program, they could find their own passwords, too.

He took this idea a bit further and wrote a BASIC program that would PEEK at the password of any account that ran the program. Thus, whenever people ran Top Secret, they were unwittingly helping the hacker find their passwords. The hacker also set up the program so that it would store all of these passwords in a file—all he had to do was leave the system alone for a week, and harvest the passwords later by accessing this special file.

Because of the level of programming and systems knowledge required to use techniques involving memory-location manipulations, only high-level hackers, like those of the Inner Circle, would attempt such feats. Most hackers are kept busy trying to keep up with system operators at lower levels.

Memory-location manipulation can be helpful, but there is another, more powerful, possibility, in some cases: the rapid-fire method. I'm not quite sure who named this method, but "rapid fire" is accurate to some degree. To understand this method, you have to know something about the way most operating systems work.

Rapid Fire

When a user enters a command, the operating system first places the command in a holding area, a buffer, where it will sit for a few millionths of a second. The system looks at the command and says, "Does this person really have authorization to do this, or not?" Then, the command sits there a few thousandths of a second while the system runs off to check the user's authorization. When the system comes back to the command, it will have one of two possible answers: "OK, go ahead," or "Sorry, get permission first."

Once you are on a system that handles things this way, you can use the rapid-fire method to change the command while it's sitting in the buffer, waiting to be executed. If you can do this, you can do anything. You can enter a command that you know will be approved, such as "tell me the time." As soon as the system runs off to verify your right to know the time, you change the command in the buffer to something you know would not be approved – perhaps "give me a list of all the passwords." When the system comes back with an "OK, go ahead," it responds to your second command, not the first.

Of course, this exchange has to be done very rapidly, but most systems existing today *can* be fooled by this trick. The question is, how easy is it to do, and how much authority do you need? I know of one system that let this one slip.

I had an account on a VAX that was used by a large corporation, a company that had many contracts with the United States Department of Defense. I thought it would be nice to gain access to the corporation's intra-company network, because I would then have access to many different computers. My account was, of course, not authorized to link to the network that I wanted to use.

This system was a bit overused, and therefore was a little more vulnerable than most to attack by the rapid-fire technique: Its capabilities were taxed, so its response time was relatively slow. Knowing this, I wrote a program, in the computer language known as C, that would replace the command in the buffer with the VMS SET HOST command that would allow me to use the company's network. Once that program was written, all I had to do was issue a command that I had authority to issue, run my program between the time the system authorized my request and the time the system actually executed it, and there I had it: access to the entire network.

This would be like sending a message in to your boss, asking for his permission to get a drink of water. When the paper comes back, with your boss's signature saying that you have authority to get a drink, you change the text of the message so that it says that you have authority to take the week off – with pay. As obvious as this tactic might seem, it worked quite well for my purposes.

Remote Sysop   The remote-sysop method of security cracking is possible on only a few systems. It requires a program that will allow one user of the target computer system to send messages to another user on the same system. In this particular case, the message sender is the hacker, and the receiver is the system operator – or rather, the system operator's terminal. The goal: fooling the computer into thinking that you are the sysop. The details are somewhat complicated, but this trick works for a very simple reason. When someone logs onto a computer system, the computer has to assume that any information coming from that terminal is being typed by the authorized owner of the account; the computer has no way to tell the real user from an impostor.

If a message-sending program already exists on the system, the hacker must modify it a little bit so that it will work for him. If there is no such program, the hacker may well decide to write his own. In fact, from an advanced hacker's point of view, it's probably best if there is no established program for this type of message exchange.

However he gets it, once the hacker has a program that can send messages to people, he can start putting the first stages of the remote-sysop scheme into action. He begins by finding out what terminal the system operator is logged onto. This is normally very simple, because the system tells you if you ask: On a DEC-10, and on many other systems, the command is SYSTAT; on VMS and several other systems, the command is SHOW USERS.

Once the hacker knows which terminal is the system operator's, he can then get down to business. If you are not familiar with computers, some of these details may seem rather confusing, so I will take the chance of overexplaining what happens next.

First, the hacker sets up his own account in a special way: He fixes it so that the operating system will not interpret his pressing the return key as what is known as a *delimiter*. When you press the return key (or any other key) on a computer keyboard, that keystroke is translated into the appropriate ASCII code. Normally, the operating system interprets the return-key code as the end of something: If there is one return, that means the end of a user-to-computer command, such as ERASE FILE <RETURN> or LOG OFF <RETURN>. During a remote sysop, if the return key is followed by another special character, for example, a combination of the Control key and the letter J, the operating system may interpret the Control-J sequence rather than the Return key as the end of a user-to-user message. In this case, Control-J is the delimiter.

When the hacker tells the operating system NOT to interpret his return key as a delimiter *while he is typing,* what he is actually doing is incorporating both a command and the "now go carry it out" signal within a message – a message that he sends to the system operator's terminal, which then carries out the "message" as the command it actually represents.

By forcing the message-passing program to take a return keystroke as data and send it to the system operator's terminal, the hacker gains the power to do anything the system operator can do – to assign passwords, erase files, create accounts, grant levels of power to individual users, even remove every account and file on the system. One of the common things to do, once you seize control of the system operator's terminal, is change his own password and log him out. When the system operator is one who is known to be hostile, hackers take particular delight in pulling this prank. Another popular sequence of commands forces the operator to grant operator powers to the account the hacker is on at the moment.

In one instance, there was a UNIX system running on a supermini belonging to a large oil company. I got to know the system operator quite well and, during one of our early chats, I mentioned that I would like to gain superuser (system operator) status. The sysop said, "Well, I'm not going to give things like that away, but if you should happen to 'acquire' superuser status on your own without my help (which is impossible), I don't suppose I could stop you, could I?" Naturally, that was a direct challenge. I pulled a remote-sysop tactic a few nights later, and I was a superuser for three months before he found out about it. This particular trick worked on this particular version of UNIX. It would not, for technical reasons, work on most others.

The Trapdoor

A trapdoor is a set of special instructions embedded in the large program that is the operating system of a computer. A permanent, hopefully secret "doorway," these special instructions enable anyone who knows about them to bypass normal security procedures and to gain access to the computer's files. Although they may sound sinister, trapdoors were not invented by hackers, although existing ones are certainly used by hackers who find out about them.

A trapdoor is originally set up by someone who is either on the system or is one of the people who created it. If you saw the movie *WarGames,* you may recall that the young hacker stumbled over a hidden code word, *Joshua,* that the system's creator had embedded in the computer's operating system. Joshua was a trapdoor – a rather unrealistic example, but nevertheless one of the more accurate hacker secrets portrayed in that movie. A real-life trapdoor is not likely to be an invitation to play with a war machine – at least not on the hacker level. In fact, I once came across a computer in which a trapdoor was used for something like poetic justice. This computer had a games account on it. The problem was, there were no games on that system worth playing. I was looking around the files that were kept under the games account, and discovered that the account itself was a very high-level account. As it turned out, this account was set up by the system operators because their boss insisted on having a higher-level account than theirs. They gave him one, but they set up this games account to keep an eye on him. He never thought to check the security of the games account.

A perfect trapdoor would be impossible to detect, and it would allow the person using it to log onto the system even if the system operators cleaned out every account and started all over, from scratch. This type of trapdoor, as far as I know, can only be planted by a person who is or was directly responsible for creating the software used in the operation of the target computer system.

It is very possible that, somewhere, there is a system that will let you onto any account you wish by entering MY*LITTLE#SECRET as a password. Almost anything is possible if the system programmer or the system operator is involved – even an account that would leave no record of its existence in the normal files and that could, consequently, be used quite freely, and for virtually any purpose. I've spent many hours in conversation with system operators and system programmers, and I would venture to guess that every large computer system in the world has some type of trapdoor built into it. Even video games and personal-computer software have trapdoors built into them. Trapdoors are just the kind of temptation that a programmer is utterly incapable of resisting.

A trapdoor set up by a hacker usually is not as effective or power-ful as those created by system programmers or system operators, un-less the hacker had access to an operator account. Normally, a hacker's trapdoor is something as simple as a second account that he never uses. Or sometimes a hacker may set the system's electronic-mail program to send the system operator a letter four months in the future, asking the sysop to set up a new account. (Most mail systems allow you to create a letter and then instruct the system to post it at a specified later date.) In that way, the operator may set up the requested account after the hacker has been found and thrown off the system.

Advanced hackers tend not to worry too much about setting up their own trapdoors, unless they have very powerful accounts. If they worry about trapdoors at all, they try to find those that were left by a powerful user. It is easier to exploit a known trapdoor than it is to cre-ate one from scratch. Novices stay away from trapdoors because they rarely know where such things are located in the operating system's programming code, and they usually don't know how to handle trap-doors, even if they are able to find them.

The Trojan Horse

A Trojan horse works much like the original wooden statue that the Greeks presented at the walls of Troy – it is an attractive or innocent-looking structure (in this case, a program) that contains a hidden trick, a trick in the form of buried programming code that can give a hacker surreptitious entry to the system that unknowingly invites the Trojan horse within its figurative walls.

The Trojan horse is very simple in theory, but also very effective when it works. The program that is written or modified to be a Trojan horse is designed to achieve two major goals: First, it tries to look very innocent and tempting to run, and second, it has within itself a few high-security tasks to try. A Trojan-horse program must be run by a user, and one whom the hacker hopes is a relatively powerful user on the target system. The effectiveness of a Trojan horse program de-pends on the fact that certain users can accomplish certain security-related tasks, while the system will stop other, nonauthorized, users. If a "normal-security" user tries to give himself a very powerful position in the system's hierarchy, the computer stops him. But if the system

94

operator tries to give the same user this position, the computer won't question the move.

Once again, a hacker must have an account on the system he wants in order for this trick to work but, as you've seen, it is normally no problem for the hacker to get a low-security account on a system. Once he has this account, he either writes a new program or modifies an existing program to turn it into a Trojan horse.

If a normal user tries to run the program, it won't do anything to help the hacker; but if the owner of a very high-security account runs the program, the power allotted to that account will enable the hidden code in the program to perform some high-security task the hacker wants done. This task will probably create a new and powerful account for the hacker, or it will give the hacker's existing account a new, higher-security status. If the program is well written, the person who ran it will never know that he has helped a hacker.

In terms of privileges and levels of security, the system operator is the most powerful user on a computer. So, if the system will allow it, a hacker tries to modify one of the system operator's files as a Trojan horse. Assuming that this would work, the diagram on the following page outlines the steps that a hypothetical Trojan horse would take if the hacker modified a system operator's file. (The system file chosen for the example calculates the amount of memory available to a user.)

In most cases, however, Trojan horses have to look like a game of some sort. This way, the hacker can write a short, but interesting, game that he hopes will interest the system operator. In one case that involved the Inner Circle, the trick was very well done.

The incident took place on a VAX located in Canada. The owner used this computer for some type of statistical or demographics work, but I was using it to teach some of our members about VMS, its operating system. We had a small bulletin-board program set up, and we would "meet" there every now and then to try out VMS. After a while we were discovered, of course, but one of our members managed to strike a deal with the operators.

Among the VAX's programs, there was a chess program. It was agreed that the operators would use it to play a game of chess against the hacker, one move a day. If the chess program (the operators) won,

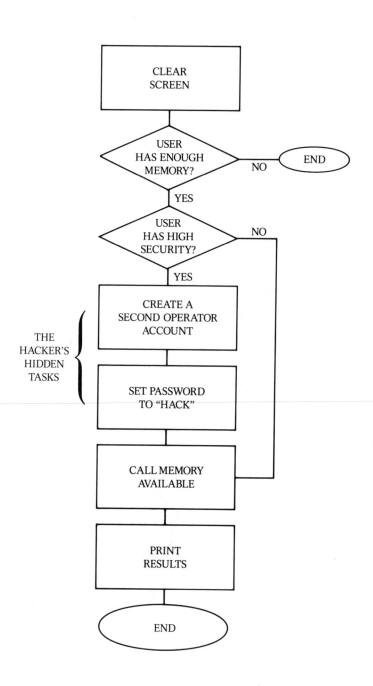

the Inner Circle would leave. But if the hacker managed to win, they would play another game, and the Inner Circle would be allowed to stay on the computer while the game was in process.

As you've no doubt guessed, the hacker turned the chess program into a Trojan horse. He had made sure the system operators had a reason to run this particular program . . . and he also altered it. Each time the system operators ran the chess game to make their daily moves, that same "innocent" program made the hacker's current account more powerful. The hacker figured that if the sysops were going to let a computer help them win at chess, he could make the game work both ways.

Logic Bombs

An operating system is a fiendishly complicated piece of programming code, and not even experts are able to determine what every single instruction in a complex operating system is intended to do. Because of this, clever programmers have the power to embed their own secret programs in any operating systems they create. A trapdoor is the most common example, and is simply a hidden subprogram that allows the system programmer to enter the system any time he wants to do so. A logic bomb is a more potent variation of the trapdoor.

Like the trapdoor, a logic bomb is a bit of programming code planted or built into a system — but a logic bomb can instruct the computer to do far more dangerous things than simply provide free access. For example, one communications software program is supposed to have a certain feature in it: If the program is sent a sequence of three control characters, in a certain order, it will return to the sender the serial number of the software. And it is rumored that the programmer of this software has a way to destroy illegal copies of his program from a remote location. Here's the connection: The rumor is that he uses the first logic bomb (the control-character sequences), via bulletin-boards, to check for pirated versions of his telecommunications program, and that he uses the second logic bomb to destroy them.

This self-protection scheme aside, however, logic bombs are normally very nasty little pieces of software trickery, and they are held in utter contempt by hackers of the Inner Circle kind, who prize knowledge of computers far more than the power to destroy them. Logic bombs are very difficult to find, because they can be fairly short programs hidden away in the much longer and more complex operating system of the target computer. Often, they are built into the software of a computer system by one of the programmers who designed it. Sometimes, and this is a particularly threatening feature of logic bombs, they can be inserted and/or triggered remotely, like timed devices activated via long-distance telephone. And this capability raises the potential for one of the worst possible outcomes of an unwanted invasion: the malicious and irreversible destruction of computer files, carried out by a vandal who is probably hundreds of miles away and is almost always totally anonymous and untraceable.

Just as a virus takes over the control mechanism of an infected cell and uses the cell's own biological machinery to do its damage, a logic bomb is capable of fooling the infected computer into erasing selected files – or even all the files that are stored online (under the control of the computer's central processor). In the case of financial information, this kind of erasure could mean the loss of millions or billions of dollars. On the other hand, suppose the computer files contained information on, let's say, patient medication records in a cancer-research hospital. The loss then would be measured in terms of human suffering, rather than dollars.

Logic bombs are feared, and correctly so, by the people responsible for the integrity of some of the most valuable computer data in the world. Whereas a Trojan horse allows access to high-security commands, and a trapdoor program admits its creator to the system, a logic bomb is a Crasher's weapon, used to damage a system. The bomb can be set to damage the system in some way when a particular high-security user runs the program containing it. Or, it can be set to detonate if a certain special condition appears or occurs.

Suppose, for example, there were a system programmer who was very, very good at creating operating systems. Every computer needs an operating system, and since every company's needs differ, a customized version of the standard operating system must be created for every large computer installation. It is often the case that these systems, or significant parts of them, are created by one person – for our purposes, our very, very good programmer.

Assume, now, that this person was responsible for customizing an extremely complicated operating system and knew that a virtually undetectable program slipped into that system would ensure his own job security. Would such a programmer be tempted? As you'll see, more than one system programmer has fallen for this temptation.

Although I and the other members of the Inner Circle always avoided and dissociated ourselves from destructive pranks, we still heard the stories. One of the standard stories that system operators like to tell their favorite hackers late at night was recently discussed by Peter J. Ognibene, in an article entitled "Computer Saboteurs" (*Science Digest*, July 1984), detailing "several incidents in which people who were fired managed to slip into the payroll software a new instruction, which said, in effect, 'When a certain name is deleted from the payroll, delete all other names and records.' The name mentioned was, of course, that of the recently fired employee."

Ognibene also mentioned another variety of logic bomb hackers sometimes talk about, a program created not by an employee, but by a company that creates commercial software: "Some software vendors put logic bombs in programs they lease. Then, if the customer fails to pay the renewal fee on time, the software self-destructs. Other cases involve former employees who put disruptive logic bombs in software they are working on just before they leave a company. Then they go into business for themselves, selling similar programs that are, of course, bug-free." Individual software authors, like the telecommunications programmer mentioned earlier, have also been known to use logic bombs in commercial programs they have created.

But the scariest aspect of logic bombs, to my way of thinking, is that they could be delivered and triggered by a hacker. It is true that there is always something to fear from any system programmer who is in a position to know more about an operating system than anybody else. But there is usually only one, or a very small group of people in this category, and their identities are known. There are hundreds, perhaps thousands, of hackers with modems, however, and those few who are crashers, and the fewer still who are clever enough to build an undetectable logic bomb, pose a very real danger to any computer system that is accessible via common-carrier communication lines.

The only way to be absolutely certain that an outsider hasn't planted a logic bomb in your computer is to be absolutely certain that outsiders are unable to get into your system in the first place. I'll discuss these countermeasures in detail in Chapter Seven.

Worm Programs

Worm programs are different things to different people. To science-fiction fans, the term may bring to mind a program that reproduces itself so fast it is impossible to destroy. But by my definition, a worm program is more straightforward. It is simply a program that is installed into the system so that whenever the system is brought up, the worm program is run along with many others. It runs without a terminal, under a name that fits right into the system operator's idea of what *should* be there, and is never found out unless (or until) it purges itself. In my opinion, the single attribute that makes a program a worm program is the fact that it does not use a single account like users do – it uses only "unused" computer resources.

When a computer can handle, say, a hundred different users, there is a tendency for that system to waste a lot of its time. A computer system is set up to divide its time among its various jobs. Every terminal hooked up to the system represents one job that the system has to take some time out to handle, even if there is no one using that terminal at the moment. If there is no one using a particular terminal, the system is wasting its time by just "waiting" for someone to use the terminal. A worm program takes advantage of some of this wasted time, and operates on the slack of everyone else's computing power.

Some types of worms must be run in many different "segments," with each segment having the information needed to rebuild a few of the preceding and following segments – much as cells contain the DNA needed to build new skin, bones, even whole bodies. Worm programs are unobtrusive, low-priority programs that run on "extra" time, so there is a possibility that a normal program may suddenly require part of the memory that is being used by the worm segment. This pre-empting would damage or destroy the segment, and require another segment to rebuild the damaged one in order to continue. Other worm programs, however, are entirely self-contained. They are also more traceable, because they reserve the memory that they need to use.

100

Recently, on a public bulletin-board system, a discussion about a very special species of "worm" broke out. During the course of this discussion, the following story was told by a person who prefers not to be named. I cannot absolutely guarantee the truth of this story, but I do know from experience with more benign versions of this program that the technical principles are valid.

According to this anecdote, which is well known to most hackers, a computer owned by a very large bank suddenly showed that over $70 million was missing. During an investigation of the problem, it became apparent that the money had actually been missing for several months, and that the embezzlement, if that's what it was, must have started as long as four or five years earlier, when the computer was first installed. The people handling the investigation couldn't be positive, but the only thing they could figure was that an undetected program had been created and set loose in the system in order to take very small amounts of money from a large number of accounts and/or deposits and add its "take" to an account or accounts belonging to the thief. The program must have been designed to cover the missing money actively by shifting funds wherever needed. Its final act was to erase itself – an event that triggered the alarms, because the monetary imbalance was no longer being covered up.

Although there is a slim chance that the story is apocryphal, such a program – that can roam through a large computer system, gathering and shifting data (or money) without adding any detectable workload to the system – is indeed possible. Although I have not worked at this scale, I have seen smaller-scale worms do the same kind of thing that would need to be done if such an embezzlement scam were to be accomplished.

The instances of worm programs that I know about were cases in which groups of hackers used this technique to assign themselves accounts. But here is an example of one of the true dangers of hackerdom: While most of the masters of this technique are not embezzlers, but rather trespassers who seek nothing more than undetected access to computing resources, less honest or more malicious people in possession of the secrets of worm programming could do a great deal of damage to a system.

One especially unpleasant aspect of worm-program penetrations is the fact that nobody ever has to know about them, although their effects are quite real. Because the most sophisticated worm programs are deliberately designed to self-destruct, there are undoubtedly more examples of successful programs than anyone will ever know about. By their nature, computer crimes committed via successful worm programs are often crimes that go undetected for years, if not forever.

CHAPTER SIX

How Much to Worry About Security

How accessible and attractive is your system to hackers? How much is the information your system contains worth to you and others? Once you can answer these questions, you will be able to determine how much trouble and expense you should go to in order to provide adequate security for your system.

The cost and extent of computer security is really a question of balance. Several factors (discussed later in this chapter) have to be weighed against each other. Even banks design their security systems knowing in advance that these systems can be violated. But rather than try to make their security one-hundred percent effective, they try to reach a balance point. Beyond this point, their cost for tighter security will be higher than if they leave their security as-is and risk losing some money to robberies. And according to Wisconsin Congressman F. James Sensenbrenner, Jr., as quoted in a July 25, 1984 Associated Press story, these losses are almost $47 million a year. Still, unless your security requirements are special (for example, the fiscal responsibilities of a bank or credit union, or the sensitive information handled by an intelligence agency or the military), you can do very well for yourself by being ninety percent hacker-proof. By my estimate, most systems today are only about forty percent hacker-proof.

COMPUTER
SYSTEMS IN
GENERAL

Computers are becoming increasingly common in the worlds of business and government. They are not yet the mainstay of the "electronic office," but wherever you turn, computers are being used more and more. From micros to supercomputers, these machines are taking on tasks from processing words to designing bridges and buildings, from tracking accounts receivable to creating theoretical models of the birth of the universe.

With so many possible applications and so many different kinds of computers, it stands to reason that there are many ways in which computer systems can be set up or used. Everything depends on what you want to do, how you want to do it, and what you choose to do with it. In order to understand how easy – or how difficult – any one of this vast array of potential system configurations might be, we need to look at the most common ways computer systems are set up, along with the ways they are accessed, and by whom.

IS YOUR
SYSTEM EASY
TO CRACK?

The first thing to evaluate in looking at your security needs is the accessibility of your system. Since most hacking is done from a distance, via modem, companies that find it possible to keep their computers off the outside phone systems altogether also find that their external security problems are at a definite minimum. If, on the other hand, companies must use one of the large public-access networks (these include UNINET, Telenet, Tymnet, and Autonet), or if the companies provide computer access for users via WATS lines (Wide Area Telecommunication Service) or 1-800 numbers, I would guess they can expect anywhere from one to one hundred hackers a month to try their luck and skill on the system involved.

It's not hard to figure out why, either. Most hackers, like users who stick to one-letter passwords or system operators who maintain lax security precautions, are lazy. They never bother to try systems they don't "stumble" upon. So, simply place yourself in the hacker's shoes and ask yourself how much trouble it would be for an outsider to find your system. A few hackers will try to locate computers through contacts within the phone company or within the computer-owning company itself, but most of them by far will be content to be kept busy by the many computers that seem to throw themselves out at hackers.

Of course, many companies need to make their computers easy to find in order to give their users as much flexibility as possible to call in. Perhaps these companies have many offices across the country, or their employees need frequent access to company files, or, as an extreme example, they may be companies whose business is selling or leasing computer time. In these cases, accessibility is an understandable necessity, but it's important to realize that this accessibility is achieved at a cost: privacy. Other companies, those that do not need this kind of public presence, have much higher levels of security, simply because they are more difficult to find and call.

In addition to phone access, you must also consider the terminals in the company buildings. Terminals are direct lines to your computer. And the more terminals you have, the easier it is for a hacker to use them without being noticed. By this, I mean something as simple and audacious as entering the building and sitting down at a vacant terminal. Hackers don't always hack by modem, anonymously and in the middle of the night. A hacker can, in some cases, spend hours at a terminal in some back office of a large company without being noticed. Or, perhaps, he can work in an office where the employee is out.

Access from Within

In other cases, the hacker may be able to use an account if a legitimate user hasn't logged off yet.... Suppose Jack Smith is a legitimate user. He decides to check his electronic mail before he leaves for the day, so he logs onto the company computer. After reading his mail, he rushes out the door so that he won't be late for his weekly poker game – forgetting to log off in his haste. Later that evening, a hacker walks in with the night shift. He finds Jack's "open" terminal and uses Jack's account as an entry into the company's system. To the computer, the hacker and Jack Smith are one and the same person.

105

Preposterous? A hacker's tale? No. The fact is, I know this can be done; several of my friends have done it – and I have done it myself.

More interesting than my story, however, is one I heard from a friend who went into a large office building with the intention of using the pay phone. When he got there he thought, "Why use a pay phone? I'm sure there are hundreds of phones upstairs I can use. And they won't cost me anything." As he expected, he found that most of the people were out to lunch and none of those who were in the building paid any attention to him. He finally found a phone that he thought he could use, and there, next to it, was a glowing terminal. He looked at the terminal and saw that an account was active on it. After playing around a little, he found that this account had quite a bit of power. He used this account to set up another one and to find out the phone number of the system. Once he got home to his own terminal, he had his very own account.

Number of Users

And what about the number of people who use your computer every day? As a general rule, the more users you have, the easier it is for a hacker to gain access to your system. One reason for this is that inside information is much easier to obtain if many people use the system. With the hacker population growing at such a rapid rate, it is fast becoming more likely that a user on a typical system knows, or knows of, someone who is a hacker. A second, perhaps more important, reason that having a lot of users will help hackers is that, as I've mentioned, users are the weakest link in the security chain. More users mean more weak links, and more weak links mean greater chances for a hacker's success. The MegaCar main computer described at the beginning of this book is a good example of both these factors.

I used MegaCar's research computer, a VAX, to show you a simplified example of what hacking is like. This special-purpose VAX would not see many users in a typical day, but the main computer of such a company might get at least a hundred and fifty different users every day. Let's assume (for the sake of argument) that one of the many people authorized to use this very busy computer knew someone who knew someone who had a brother who was a hacker. Let's also assume that this person allows – either intentionally or through

106

carelessness – his friend's friend's brother to get hold of the information required to use the computer.

Now a hacker has the information, which became available in the first place because of the large number of users with access to Mega-Car's computer. What would happen if that one hacker started playing around with the system? And what would happen if he gave the access information to twenty of his cohorts? The operators would have a hard time spotting the activities of these hackers, with a hundred and fifty people logging in and out of the computer all the time. But twenty-one unknown snoops, with no compunction to keep MegaCar's access information private, would be free to go their merry ways.

By now, you may have a pretty good idea of the accessibility of your system. Keep that in mind as you go on to examine your system's attractiveness, or "value," to an average hacker. Since a hacker has literally tens of thousands of systems to choose from, he is not likely to spend too much time on a system in which he doesn't have any interest. It's quite difficult to evaluate the attractiveness of your system, because of the wide range of possible motives hackers might have, but many systems seem to appeal needlessly to all hackers, and this can, and should, be avoided. The following descriptions will give you an idea of systems that seem to attract a lot of hackers.

IS YOUR SYSTEM ATTRACTIVE TO HACKERS?

Systems with many users. Let's assume that Solid State has run across four different systems today. He wants to spend a few hours trying to get onto one of them, and of course he wants the best possible chance of succeeding in this limited time. If one of these four new systems has an unusually large number of users, he will spend his time on that one.

Solid State may be able to find the number of users on the system from the welcome message, or from the way the system acts when he calls it. Or, the system may accept limited commands before he is logged on – commands that will allow him to get this information.

Systems that handle hundreds or thousands of users every day are vulnerable systems, and very likely to attract hackers. One of the major reasons for this, as I mentioned earlier, is the fact that users are the weakest link in most computer systems' security, and the added users provide more weak links. Another aspect of these systems that makes them attractive to hackers is the fact that their operators are busy and don't have nearly as much time to worry about security as the sysops on less congested machines.

Well-known companies. Slasher the Crasher is calling systems. He spies a computer owned by a "household name," and his mouth starts to water right away. You recall we compared Crashers with vandals; both want to earn as much "fame" as possible, and Slasher the Crasher would gladly choose the well-known company over a possibly more valuable system that belongs to a company no one has heard of.

Systems belonging to well-known companies will attract not only Crashers, but more than their share of other hackers, too. Some of the hackers will choose well-known companies because they feel they are achieving more than they would by getting into equally complex computers belonging to less famous organizations. Others hope to gain publicity among other hackers, or they wish to see the files of these corporations and learn about what goes on in them. But most hackers are drawn to well-known companies only because large companies have large computers. And then, of course, there are the competing companies, which have their own motives—motives, such as piracy, or "sneaking a peek," that really are outside the scope of this book.

In addition, one of the first things novice hackers do is try to get onto the systems of the largest companies they can find. Novices shouldn't concern most companies yet, because these hackers, at their level of experience, just don't have much of a chance of getting into a reasonably secure system. Once their numbers grow, however, the volume of their attempts alone could be a big problem, even if none of the hackers gets in: The phone lines will always be busy and the computer workload will be wasted on checking passwords.

Service computers. When ProHacker wants to play a game, get stock market results, or talk to other users interested in TRS-80s, no computer will allow him to do all of these things better than a computer that exists only to provide such services. This computer probably also qualifies as a system with a large number of users, *and* as a system owned by a large company.

Many hackers who try to get into these service computers are simply trying to get the service for free, but there are rumors that a few could be out to resell computer time – most likely by selling, for a one-time fee, accounts and passwords that would last a few weeks or so until the operators found and removed them. Service computers are usually large systems, so by their nature, and because they are both well known and accessible, they automatically tend to attract a large number of hackers.

Hacker-friendly systems. After a long day of exploring computers that are totally unknown to him, a hacker likes to spend some time on a computer where the people running it welcome him. Some system operators and programmers talk to hackers on a daily basis; hackers find this quite refreshing, and probably more interesting than do the people running the system.

Systems that are known to have operators who are friendly toward hackers naturally attract hackers. The hackers learn about them through private hacker bulletin boards, and usually use these systems to talk to one another (as well as to the system operator), because they don't need to fear giving themselves away. On the surface, hacker-friendly systems may sound like a contradiction in terms, but they are surprisingly common.

University computers – the ones used by students, faculty, and the administration – quite often qualify for this category, because they are usually not used for anything that seriously needs security equipment. While the university administrators may not like the idea of hackers using the computer without proper authorization, the system operators are the only people who know who has authorization and who doesn't – and they are often students themselves. One university computer I was quite fond of had a system operator who would allow us to hack all we wanted. When we ran into trouble getting onto the system, we could just ask him and he would even give us the password to one of the professors' accounts.

"Easy" systems. Systems that are known to have security problems are quite popular with hackers, for reasons that must be obvious by now. Hackers normally keep in touch with one another about such easy systems to crack. Some are easy because the operators neglect basic security precautions; others are easy because the operating system is old and simply not as secure as the newer versions. But regardless of the reason, once such a system is discovered by one hacker, you can be sure that the word will get around to many more.

Systems on a network. Other than the services they provide, an important difference exists between a privately owned computer that is accessed via one or a few public telephone lines and a more "universal" computer that is one of several on a dial-up network. Both types of computers respond to phone calls, and both types can be explored by a hacker with a modem. The big difference is, the privately owned computer has a limited (and known) group of users and its phone numbers are not very widely known. A computer on a network, on the other hand, has a much larger group of users (think of THE SOURCE, for example) and there is no limit to the number of people who know the phone number needed to access it.

As I've mentioned throughout this book, systems on large public networks are likely to get a lot of hacker activity. Hackers can almost always call the network easily toll-free, and the chance of being traced through the network is very slim, if the hacker knows what he is doing.

Networks have been described in various ways by hackers, but I think the best description came from a hacker known as The Wizard of ARPANET, who said, sometime in early 1982, "Networks are a hacker's fantasy." Of course, at that time, networks provided hackers with a real dreamworld: thousands of computers, accessible by phone, that had no better security, and thus were no more difficult to access, than any other computer. But now, since the number of hackers is growing so fast, the security of most systems on networks gets a healthy test as soon as the computer is put on the network.

In fact, network computers are often more secure than many privately owned computers with phone links, just because more hackers quickly find and test the network's defenses. These days, hackers more often spend their time "scanning" phone numbers, hoping to find a private computer, than they do searching for a way through the tighter security barriers of a well-guarded network system. As I said, hackers are lazy (at least at this level of hacking) and would just as soon bump into an easily breached system.

All this, however, doesn't mean to say that the owner or user of a network computer has no security worries at all. There are still a lot of hackers trying a lot of different computers, and some hackers are very good and very dedicated (remember the Tourist?). Some hackers are bound to get on some networks, and once they are there, it sometimes happens that the hacker doesn't have to be anything but persistent and likable to go farther. . . . For example:

Sometimes, when exploring on a network, a hacker will come across an address (a remote computer) that seems dead. No matter what he types, the distant machine just sits there. Quite often, however, when this happens, the hacker can type in HELLO???, enter a few Control-Gs (the character that makes a bell ring on the terminal at the other end), and someone will reply. If this happens, the other person is almost always someone in a computer room, and depending on who that person is, and where his sympathies lie, the hacker can sometimes talk him into helping out with an account or a password. In this case, hacking is a lot like walking up and ringing a doorbell. If this can happen on your system, make sure your sysops know how to say "No."

No one wants to give away free computer time, but is security really worth $5000, plus $350 a user? Or $12,000, plus $600 a user? In the vast majority of cases, the answer is no. Despite all the recent quantum leaps in technology, we are not yet out of the ink-and-paper age. Computers are still an adjunct, and computer information is usually backed up several times, in more than one medium, for safekeeping. In terms of potential destruction of data, this backup process simply means that computers do not justify security as a major expense. If you want to keep your system safe from Crashers or bungling amateur hackers, I think that rather than spending a large amount of money on security, you could probably do much better by educating your users on keeping personal accounts secure.

On the other hand, suppose your concerns are with the security of confidential information, or as I mentioned at the beginning of this chapter, finances – computer information that represents actual dollars that belong to someone. In this case, you not only need to back up

THE SECURITY BALANCE

111

the information for historical purposes, you need to keep outsiders from seeing the contents of your files. You really may need to consider going to some expense to protect your system.

The security balance, as I described for banks, is a seesaw – a tradeoff – between the expense of tightening your security and the estimated expense of your potential losses if you leave your security at a lower level. When the cost of your security exceeds your losses, it's time to sit back and re-evaluate what you want and what you need. You don't need a cannon to protect your home, and you don't need *007* security tactics to protect your accounts receivable. What you *do* need is to figure out the value of your data on your system: Just how much are all those numbers and letters that go through your computer every day worth to you, and to others?

Here is a list of questions to consider in evaluating your own situation and your own security requirements:

How secret is the information that is kept or managed on the system? Would the data, although it may not mean that much to you, be of use to a competitor? Some information can be very valuable to a competing company.

In a case reported by security expert Donn Parker, there were two companies that would bid against each other on various projects. The company with the lowest bid got the job. During a period of several months, one of the companies underbid the other one-hundred percent of the time – there was only a very slight chance this could ever happen out of sheer coincidence.

Eventually, it was discovered that the "winning" company had access to the other company's computer system. It was able to find out how much the "losing" company was planning to bid on all its projects, and could then plan to underbid by a very small amount.

How "solid" are these numbers on the computer? Do you back up your data well? Do you have time to check online data against backed-up data often? Or do you take what the computer says for granted? If you can't easily spot hacker-changed data, then you may be working with incorrect figures and not even know it. Certain credit bureaus may operate for years without checking computer data against anything in the "real world," for instance.

Or suppose the numbers on your computer system change by the hour—perhaps you list the current stock market prices for the top 100 stocks and update them every hour. If the information is to be updated in ten minutes, and you need to know the price of one of the stocks now, you will take the word of the computer. After all, the computer exists to let you know the most current price, and if you had to verify the price by calling New York why use the computer? Since you take the numbers coming from this system for granted, you should spend effort in making sure your security keeps them correct.

What is the dollar value of the data to the public? Could you charge $250 an hour to access your data base? If you could—if your information is that valuable and that much in demand—and if your security is not high enough, perhaps someone *is* charging the public $250 an hour.... Check the accounts and activity on your system.

DIALOG, for example, is a very large computer database service owned by Lockheed. At one time, the data bases incorporated into DIALOG were separate and privately owned, but the owning companies decided to charge outside users for access to their data bases. Some now cost the public in the hundreds of dollars an hour to access. Any information is worth something. And if it's marketable, it may be worth quite a lot.

How much weight should you give to the time that hackers may spend on your system? Computer time itself is worth money. It is up to you to determine just how much your system's time is worth, not only in terms of offsetting the cost of equipment and operating expenses, but also in terms of productivity. For example, I know of a hacker who once accidentally started a batch process that ended up costing tens of thousands of dollars in computer time before it was through. Oops.

How much computer time do you need? If you are pushing the limits of your system already (and many companies are), then you can't afford to allow several hackers the chance to move around unnoticed. If nothing else, they will probably demand more time than an average user, because they search the disks so much. Then, too, if Hammer decides to set up a hacker's bulletin-board system on your mainframe, and seventy people call every day, they can be quite a strain on your system. If your system is finding it tough enough to deal with authorized users, you don't need to donate twenty-five percent of its time to the "hacker's cause."

How much is your computer worth? Some computer time sells for hundreds of dollars a minute. If you have a fast or otherwise advanced computer, then you need to protect its time. Once again, if you don't, some invisible entrepreneur may do it for you. Just as a general scale of measurement, try to decide what the cost of your computer time would be if you were to sell it to the public. In some cases, two or three dollars an hour would be too much, while in others, two or three dollars a minute would be very cheap. If just a few minutes a day adds up to quite a bit of money, it may be worth a little extra expense to ensure that hackers stay off your system.

Does your system control any external devices? While this question applies to a specialized group of people, there are some computers responsible for controlling such devices as phone services and printing presses. Damage or misuse of such devices compounds the expense and headaches associated with abuse of the computer alone, so these systems usually have to have the best security possible. The program "60 Minutes" did a story some years ago, about a group of kids who found some information on a telephone-company computer system and ended up with the power to shut off phone service to millions of Los Angeles residents. That computer system should never have been on the phone lines.

USE YOUR SYSTEM TO DISCOURAGE HACKERS

It is always best to prevent a hacker from ever intruding on your system in the first place. If you remove him after he has been on for a number of hours or days, he has had a good chance to look at your security from the inside, to acquire plenty of account names, and (if he's a high-level hacker) to set up some type of logic bomb or Trojan horse. As you saw in Chapter Five, these tricks are designed either to help the hacker or to harm the system *after* he has been thrown off your computer. Sometimes, long after.

It could be that, by now, you've decided your system security is adequate for your current needs. On the other hand, you may feel you need some extra security, but of course that's going to take a little time. In either situation, you're still interested in keeping hackers off your system *now*. If a hacker manages to gain access to your system, how can you discourage him?

In many cases where system security is not a high priority, the operator tries to handle some security operations manually. It is almost always all right for the operator to hang up on a hacker manually (the hacker assumes the system is doing so). But no matter whether the operator or the system can hang up on the hacker, it is often a mistake for an operator to break in and try to talk to him.

Suppose the hacker tries ten or twelve passwords to an account, and then the system operator breaks in to say something like "Go away," "What do you want with this system?" or "I've just traced your number. The FBI is on the way." In a few cases, this move will be successful but, in most situations, these confrontations will only incite the hacker to bigger and better efforts. If the hacker doesn't decide to leave, he may consider the operator's words as a personal challenge.

Now, you may well be asking yourself, "Why should I care if a hacker thinks he's been challenged?" Because hackers have one thing going for them that should make you care: a very quick and easy mode of communication. Here is an example of what can happen if they decide to use this advantage.

A hacker calls ZZXY's computer and casually tries a few level-one things off the top of his head. Then, for some reason, he decides to keep trying at this computer – perhaps he likes the way the system "looks," or he thinks the security will be lax. Soon after he gets interested in the system, an operator breaks in and tells the hacker to leave the system alone. As I said, at this point many hackers would leave the system, thinking that the security here must be fairly high if an operator has time to be catching and talking to hackers. But bear in mind that many hackers are competitive (at least on their own "turf") and are quite likely to think of hacking as something of a game, like chess. So, let's assume this hacker decides he must get into the system, to "beat" the operator. This attitude surfaces quite often, and presents you with two dangers:

First, the hacker will spend more effort on the system; he is no longer thinking, "It would be nice to get into that system." Now he is thinking, "I *must* get into that system." And because he wants to beat the operator, he is also likely to enter the system in a way that won't be so easily detected, because he knows he is under observation.

But the second danger is the more serious of the two. The hacker may decide to start using various computer bulletin-board systems across the country to communicate with other hackers. He will ask many different hackers for help in breaking into your system.

To illustrate the consequences of this second problem, here's one case that I know of. A hacker had gained access to a computer. The system operator broke in and told the hacker that his number had been traced and he was to leave right away, or the police would be called. The hacker agreed to go, but said that, unless the system operator could prove that he had traced the hacker's number, he would come back later. The hacker knew that phone numbers must be traced with the help of the phone company, and that the process takes time and advance preparation. The sysop was almost certainly bluffing, so the hacker wanted the operator either to type his phone number or name over the computer, or to send the police within a few days.

Of course the system operator had not traced the number, so the hacker called back. But the next time, he had friends with him. Over a hundred of them. I think that this company had to get rid of its modem lines because of this.

A SECURITY CHECKLIST

I should mention here that most systems in use today *should* be considered quite secure and *would* be if they were run as they were designed to be run. Security is easier to neglect on some systems than it is on others, but most systems have many passive security tools that the users are free to use—or to ignore.

Certain systems have little quirks or tendencies that may make life easier for a hacker, but the real responsibility for security belongs to the users and the operators. A system may enable a hacker to see who is logged on before he starts hacking, but it is the *users* who choose passwords that the hacker finds so easy to guess. A system may make it easy to go with certain well-known defaults, but it is the system operator or programmer who decides to use them. Just as people may go out at night, leaving doors or windows open in their houses, users and operators may neglect system security.

But, as you can see, threat or nuisance, vandals or pranksters, hackers can cause headaches if they gain access to your system. Even if you don't handle huge amounts of money or process top-secret data, your system could still attract hackers—most particularly if it's easy to access or if it's a state-of-the-art machine, the kind that hackers especially like to find. It's important to evaluate what you've got and what you need, so in light of the preceding discussions, here is a security checklist covering the most popular operating systems. This information is not based on any research study or statistical analysis. It's based on my own experiences as a hacker and on my conversations with other hackers, system operators, and system programmers. It's a hacker's impressions of system security. You might say it's the view from the other side of the modem.

UNIX

Among computer companies and computer professionals who are knowledgeable about operating systems, the term *UNIX* is generally used to refer to a number of different versions of a very popular operating environment. The name *UNIX* itself is a trademark of Bell Labs, which developed the original operating system in the late '70s. Today, however, there is UNIX itself, a number of modified, licensed versions of UNIX, and various UNIX-like operating systems that have been developed independently. In addition, because the program code in the early versions of Bell's own UNIX could be—and was—tailored to each purchaser's own system requirements, there are many unique, "homemade" variations of UNIX, as well — variations that may no longer have the original version's security safeguards. And all these different "UNIXES" run on just about any computer system . . . from a $2000 personal computer to a $700,000 IBM system.

With this operating system, it is hard to pinpoint any particular hacker "loopholes," just because so many versions exist. But here are a few common approaches:

On some versions it is possible to execute a WHO-type command at the log-on prompt. This command gives a list of the user names logged on at the time, and within certain limits tells what the users are doing. In some situations, it is helpful for an actual user to find out how many people are logged on before he or she logs on, but this information can also needlessly encourage the hacker by giving him account names and by telling him how large your system is and what type of work is done.

A user on a UNIX system is generally either a user or what is called a superuser. A user's power is essentially limited to his own file space and public access areas, while a superuser is somewhat akin to a sysop. In most UNIX systems, a "normal account" turns itself into a superuser's account by a single, password-protected command: Type something like SU (for superuser) and the system asks for a password. This could mean trouble because many different people are likely to have this password, and if reasonable security is not kept, it probably has a much greater chance of getting out than a normal sysop's account, which would be known only to perhaps two or three people.

As a general rule, UNIX-like systems are designed to keep programmers happy, and this, in many cases, keeps hackers happy too. While they may not always be vulnerable, UNIX systems are desirable and have been the favorite target of hackers who like to get things done by writing programs (such as Trojan horses or rapid-fire techniques) or generally just finding a new way to do things altogether.

The passwords in the UNIX system are kept open to every user... but in encrypted form. It is almost certainly beyond hope for anyone to try to decrypt a password, especially since the hacker must already have one account on the system. However "almost certainly" is not one-hundred percent. There have been a few attacks made on this system of keeping passwords, so you should keep this fact in mind.

TOPS and RSTS   TOPS and RSTS are operating systems designed to run on certain DEC minis and mainframes. A more user-friendly system than many, this type of system is often the target of new hackers, because it is generally quite helpful. Here are a few features that hackers use:

These systems are famous for allowing limited commands before a person is logged on. The commands usually allow a user to check who is logged on, and they sometimes allow a user to send messages or even mail of some type. Hackers can get lists of account names and can even talk to the users in hope of finding some unsuspecting someone who will give away his or her account.

This system usually uses what's called a PPN as an account name. In practice, this means that account names are two numbers separated by a comma – such as 100,104. This feature is not actually a security problem in itself, but it is worth mentioning, because quite often numbers such as 100,100 or 400,400 are set up as demonstration or open accounts, and hackers try these, just as they try DEMO on systems that use words as account names.

VMS

VMS is an operating system designed to run on a VAX computer, which is made by DEC. VMS is perhaps one of the most user-friendly systems available. Hackers also consider it one of the more secure. No commands are allowed before log on and, as far as I know, there aren't any built-in defaults a hacker can exploit. The inner-system of security also makes it easy to set up a "secure" system.

When a hacker runs across a VMS machine, he knows it because the log-on prompt is USERNAME:. To confirm his assumption he will probably hit Control-Y. If he needs further proof, he will enter a false user name with a /XXXX on the end, and then the same false user name with a /COMM = XXXX on the end. A VMS machine should give an error for the first entry, and allow the second.

Once he establishes that this *is* a VMS machine, the hacker is pretty much on his own. He will try many things, such as DEMO and GAMES, because a surprising number of VMS machines seem to have these accounts. The system also makes it easy to default the password to "same as user name," so hackers will often try that, too. Last, though I have never been able to confirm this, I have been told that on VMS there is a sequence of characters (Control and otherwise) that would allow anyone to access a maintenance mode that is quite powerful. Fact or fiction? I don't know.

Once a hacker is on a VMS machine, however, he finds this operating system very user friendly. And because it is, it is also one that is quite often used by people who are not interested in computers. The overall effect is that security may actually be weak, because the users are less interested in security.

Primos   Primos is the operating system that runs on the Prime series of super-mini and mainframe computers, of which the Prime 750 is the largest. In the past five years, Primos has moved from being one of the most non-secure systems to being probably one of the top five in security. Many (if not most) companies, however, still run the older versions of Primos, and many smaller businesses are buying used systems. Here are a few possible problems:

The earlier versions of Primos had no password system at all. A user would call the system and enter LOGIN <USERNAME> and would be in the system just that easily. If a hacker were to try LOGIN JOE and Joe were not a valid user name, the system would simply tell the hacker to try again. In one case I remember, the user names were actually that easy: On about my fifth try, I entered LOGIN STEVE, and this was a valid user name. Once I was on the system, I easily found all the other user names, too.

For these same versions of Primos, third-party companies wrote password-protection programs for the owners of Prime systems. I am sure quite a few of them are very good, but the ones that I ran across were very sloppy and easily outwitted. As you can see, such inadequate protection can lead to a false sense of security.

There was one instance in which the old Primos *did* require a password. The problem was, this password defaulted to XXXXXX (six Xs) and was very rarely changed.

All but the newest version of Primos have certain default accounts, the most famous being FAM, DOS, and SYSTEM. This means that if the system is left as-is, after it is installed by the company, someone need only enter LOGIN FAM, LOGIN DOS, or LOGIN SYSTEM to be admitted to the system.

The newest version of Primos—revision 19—is quite secure as far as I know, and any hacker would probably need to resort to some of the techniques discussed in Chapter Five in order to get anywhere. As I said, however, there are still quite a few earlier versions of these machines available to a hacker.

VM-370   VM-370 is an operating system that usually runs on an IBM-370. In most cases, VM-370 is not nearly as friendly to hackers as many other systems, so hackers don't know much about it relative to some others. Not that they couldn't get the user manuals . . . or call IBM and ask for technical help. It's just that they find it is so much easier to use one of the systems that offer a bit more help on demand.

I was told by a friend who was more informed than I that, once inside a VM-370 system, a hacker finds the system, like VMS, is quite user friendly. According to him, the difference between the DEC and IBM systems in terms of hacker-related security probably comes from one major feature: The owners of DEC machines, he believes, are encouraged more to use networks because of DECnet, a system of networking various DEC machines, both together and to public networks. And, as you know, hackers love networks, because a call to one computer enables them to access many.

IBM systems are also capable of such networking but, the company itself seems to lean more toward keeping the systems independent and off the networks. This tendency can be either good or bad, depending on how you look at it but, from a security aspect, it is good, because the hacker's world as a whole does not contact IBM systems nearly as much as it contacts other systems.

CHAPTER SEVEN

Make the Most of What You've Got

Before you go spending huge amounts of money on external security devices, why not learn the best use of all those simple, yet effective, security features that are built into most systems? If properly used, almost any system has the ability to stop almost any hacker's best efforts.

In my experience, the most effective security systems have been the ones that used multiple lines of defense – at least two methods in conjunction. Even if you have, or are considering, the best and brightest of hacker-proof security devices, it's my belief that one awesome, perfect, unfailing device cannot substitute for the combination of two or three less wonderful methods. Even if you have a state-of-the-art callback modem (which verifies a user's authorization before connecting him or her with the system), you still don't have an excuse for sloppy password security. Even if you use encryption to make your data unreadable, you'll be safer yet if you also have an unlisted, well-hidden telephone number.

A FALSE SENSE OF SECURITY

Hackers love to find a company that claims no hacker will ever see the inside of its system. In a few cases, such a claim will only serve to motivate the hacker. More often, though, and more importantly, such a claim advertises to high-level hackers that the system in question has only one line of defense – one security barrier on which the company depends completely.

Even if the claim is simply the unspoken belief of the company involved, too much reliance is still placed on a single precaution. All too often, the company with "the ultimate security system" doesn't believe that it needs to bother with all those other silly security precautions – such as secure passwords and detailed user logs. That's a mistake. As the saying goes, "don't put all your eggs in one basket."

Once, I remember, there was one company that thought it had cornered the market in security. It had a nice little computer system and allowed access to it on only one unlisted telephone line. Presumably, if no one knows you have a computer system on an unlisted phone line, then who can find out about it? Especially if you are sure that no one in the company is going to give out the number – so this company thought, anyway, and with some justification. But, because the company never expected an unauthorized user to find the computer – even by accident – there was essentially no security other than that well-hidden phone number.

One day, however, an employee stumbled upon a file created by hackers several months earlier. All told, five hackers had used this system freely for about a year before they were discovered. They had done the system no harm, but if a crasher had discovered that computer, he could easily have destroyed hundreds of hours of labor.

At the other end of the scale, I know of a very large system that needed to use a very busy network. Taking the advice of a well-paid consultant, the owners equipped the system with a state-of-the-art device for coding and decoding data (cost of device and the consultant together, more than $270,000). The device on this system required each user to use a special terminal capable of performing the necessary scrambling and unscrambling of data, and these terminals were supplied only to authorized users. On the surface, this would probably look like a very secure system. It was, but not unconquerable.

A little help from the inside (not hard to get from such a large company) and a little programming skill allowed a hacker to use his personal computer as one of these terminals. After that bit of work, the rest of the system became an open book, because no one in the company could imagine that this expensive and sophisticated security device might be circumvented. Once again, the security was very lax once the single existing barrier was overcome.

THE HUMAN FACTOR

The preceding example told of an instance in which a hacker received help from within the company whose computer he was seeking to access. Perhaps you are thinking, "Oh well, that was just a stroke of luck for the hacker." No, it wasn't. In fact, when I was recently asked, "How do hackers go about getting inside help from a large company?" my first reaction was to call that a silly question. But then I realized that if one person didn't know, there must be others who don't know either.

The larger a company is, the easier it is for a hacker to get inside help. The hacker's first advantage is that employees of a multibillion-dollar corporation quite often do not consider such a huge organization "real." The employees of such a company may charge personal, long-distance phone calls to the company, or they may take home pens, pencils, paper, and other supplies. If they don't, are they honest because of fear? Or because of respect for the company in question? The issue of employee involvement is obviously far beyond the scope of this book, but the fact remains: People who feel a sense of commitment and responsibility are far less likely to become security risks than people who see their employer as the source of a paycheck and not much more.

A secondary reason that inside help can be easy for a hacker to get in large companies is the simple fact that there are more people for him to try. In most cases, a hacker doesn't have any contacts in the company, but he will probably only have to talk to a few people before finding help. By "a few people," I mean, usually, one or two. As you can see, the odds are strongly in the hacker's favor.

Hackers (or anyone else) can, if they need to, quite easily obtain a company phone book from almost any large corporation. As another

example, assume that you work for MegaComputer, Inc., and someone calls you at your office and asks you to read a four-digit number off
a thick gray wire coming out of the wall next to your desk. He tells you
that he is from the company's maintenance department. Or maybe he
even takes a bolder approach and assures you that he is only a kid out
for fun—no harm or vandalism intended—after all, wouldn't a criminal
just break in and read the number himself? If this scenario seems unlikely, or you're sure you wouldn't fall for a "mischievous-kid" story,
why not stop and think a moment about all the times you're in a hurry
or your mind is on something else. . . . Remember, the helper isn't necessarily willing in the sense of "aiding and abetting." Ignorance and
carelessness can serve a hacker just as well.

Educating
Users

The question of developing security consciousness among users is
much harder to resolve than the problem of developing security guide-
lines for your system. How can you get users to watch out for their own
accounts if they only log on once a month and don't really care about
the system one way or the other? Users need to know how they can
help and, more importantly, why they should help. If they don't, or if
they don't care, they will just be easy targets for hackers.

Computer users need the education that will allow them to use
security systems the way they were meant to be used. They need to be
able to spot any hacker activity on their accounts; they need to know
what to do or whom to call when they suspect hacker activity; and
they need to be aware enough of security *not* to give their account and
password to anyone—not to anyone in the company, and definitely not
to that youngish-looking technician who says he's from IBM. Computer owners and system operators should take the time and effort to
educate their users. If they did, hacking as it is today would fall to such
a low level of activity it could be considered dead. It's that simple.

Failing the possibility of in-house user education, this subject is
important enough to some companies to justify the cost of sending
users to a series of classes or seminars, or of bringing in an expert to
conduct a special session on computer security. Most companies would
probably get back their investment within half a year or so . . . and a
few would profit greatly for not having lost.

Whether you choose to educate your users yourself, send them to classes, or bring in an expert, another good idea is to work out a system of assigning passwords after the user finishes the security course. As a final exam, the user can pick his or her own secure password.

But, no matter how you decide the question of educating your users, you should consider having the system itself throw out periodic reminders and suggestions on security: "Hello, John Smith. It's been over fifteen months since you changed your password. Don't you think it's about time?" or, simply, "Remember, a secure system helps us provide you with a secure job."

THE SYSTEM ITSELF

As you've seen throughout this book, hackers and users must both use a common route to gain access to a computer system: They must either use a terminal that is directly connected to the computer, or they must call in through a modem. Once they've obtained access to the system, they must then log on with accounts and passwords to be able to do any kind of work with the system.

There are different ways you can protect your system at these access points. Some are specific to terminals, some are specific to modems and phone lines, and some are general techniques that apply to both hard-wired terminals and to remote communications devices.

As I mentioned in Chapter Six, hackers are very fond of getting the maximum amount of fun from the minimum amount of effort. Almost all hackers, almost all of the time, prefer to take what systems are dangled in front of their noses. Make it difficult for hackers to stumble across, or use, your system "without really trying," and you will be well on your way to much tighter security.

Your first security measure, then, is inaccessibility.

Terminals

It's not a good idea to have a terminal in every office and several more in the lobby or in back rooms. Having a terminal in every office makes it easy, but not many hackers are really going to want to go into someone's office. When you add extra terminals in the halls or in unused rooms, however, it's like saying to a hacker, "We've got more terminals than we need; feel free to sit and use that one for a few hours or so."

All those terminals may make life easier for you, but they also mean that the users-to-terminals ratio is low, and this makes it all the easier for a hacker to find a terminal that no one uses regularly.

You also want to make sure that the system checks for activity from users. If a terminal gets no activity for more than ten minutes or so, it should be logged out automatically. If this is not done, you are going to have people leaving for lunch or possibly for the weekend and leaving their accounts active on their terminals. A hacker would only need to sit at the terminal to read the user's mail and/or to get an inside look at your system.

Phone Lines And Modems

Whether or not you have terminals scattered about the offices in your company, if you also allow phone access to your computer system, you have another set of security problems to contend with. The "classic" hacker these days seems to be an upper-middle-class teenager locked in his bedroom in the middle of the night, manipulating the system of some corporate or governmental giant thousands of miles away. Well, the portrait is somewhat exaggerated, but it is true in the sense that most hacking is done at night (when loads on the systems are lighter) and it is almost always done by phone.

If you must keep your system on the phone lines for some reason, here are a few things to keep in mind.

See if it is possible to eliminate phone-line access totally. This would be a very welcome occurrence for system operators who must worry about security. Think about whether you really need phone lines to your system and about how tight your security is. In one case, I was talking to a system operator who was not so security minded. When he asked what terminal I was working from, I shocked him by answering that I was in a different time zone than he was. He had thought that I must be in the building, because the phone lines hadn't even been used in the almost two years he had worked there. This company could easily have done without the eight or ten phone lines that were dedicated to the machine but, as far as I know, the lines are still there and still unused by employees of the company.

See if you can limit outside calls to a local telephone area. If only local hackers can call your system, you may eliminate your current or potential problems with hackers. The hackers who are local to you won't want to risk being found – the phone company has less trouble tracing regional, rather than long-distance, numbers. I should mention that most hackers would know of at least one way to get around "regional numbers." It involves using someone's PBX, and it's quite a bit of extra trouble, however, so you'll still discourage most, if not all, local hackers.

If you must *allow your users to call in from all over the country, check the possibility of taking your main computer off the outside lines and setting up a smaller, five- or ten-user system to handle the phone calls.* There are two ways you could go about this. The first, adopted from the large networks and used by some computer-owning companies with great success, allows users to call in and *send* information only. For example, suppose you are part of a large newspaper company and you must allow reporters to call in and transmit stories to your computer. Why put your multimillion-dollar computer, which is also responsible for such things as payroll and subscriptions, on the phone lines, when a nice ten-thousand-dollar system can do the job just as well? After your reporter submits a story, you can then check it and send it on to your main computer for word processing or typesetting.

The second approach to taking your main computer off the phone lines is actually much broader based, because it allows users both to send and receive information. In this case, you would still set up a small system to answer the phones, but you could put on it any non-secure files of information your users might need. For example, if your company has sales representatives throughout the country, you could keep such things as your product-catalog lists and prices on the small system. Then, whenever your people needed to check product information or, perhaps, check for messages or new leads, they could call your small system without having to access the main computer.

In both cases, you would succeed in keeping hackers away from the main system, and you would have the added advantage of presenting any possible hackers with only a small, relatively uninteresting computer to play with. There is the possibility that someone could still set up a logic bomb by sending a special program or certain characters, but this type of occurrence would almost certainly have to be an inside job, because a hacker would need to know exactly how information was handled after it was input.

Keep the modem phone number(s) unlisted. This suggestion appears to be common sense, but there really *are* a few listed modem phone numbers. In a few cases, the number is meant to be very public anyway, and the hacker doesn't need to hunt for it – either he already has the number or he can easily get it. But can you imagine being a hacker, calling up information, and saying, "I'd like the number for MegaCar. The research department, please." And hearing, "Sir, do you mean the computer or the voice line?"

If possible, keep your modem number(s) on a different three-digit exchange from that of your listed numbers. In other words, if your listed (or otherwise well-known) phone number is 555-1234, it is not a good idea to have a modem line with the number 555-8537. Even worse is a modem line with the number 555-1233 or 555-1235. A hacker may try dialing the phone numbers that are very close to the listed number of a company, for no reason other than it's something to do. If your modem number is close to your company number, he will succeed in reaching your computer. Even if the numbers are not close, a hacker who wants to get your modem number for a particular purpose can usually set his modem to call all the numbers from 0000 to 9999 for your company's exchange. If he has the modem check for the answer of another computer, he can try about one number every seven to ten seconds. If he monitors the modem calling himself, he can increase the rate to as fast as one attempt every three to five seconds.

On the other hand, if the exchange for your computer differs from the listed number of your company, the hacker is very likely to give up after scanning the company exchange – after all, while he was scanning the exchange for your computer, he probably found fifty other computers to play with.

Ask the phone company to classify your modem phone lines as voice grade, rather than the computer-only data grade. There is no difference in quality between the two as long as communications are taking place at 1200 (possibly even 2400) baud or less, and it pays to get your phone number off the infamous data-grade list. Novice hackers have been known to discover data-grade lists in telephone company trash cans, but since the only real difference in the two grades is a reference in a telephone company computer, other hackers can get hold of the lists in "cleaner" ways, too.

I know of one case in which a semi-secret government computer was very well hidden from scanning hackers. Rather than connect a caller directly with the computer on the first ring, the modem would ring three times, and a recording would then answer. After the recording was over, there was a minute pause before the computer answered. But despite these precautions, the modem was on a data-grade line, and through a reference in a phone company computer, I had been able to find the phone number and call the system. Actually, the other security seemed quite good, too, so I never tried getting in. I'm sure they spotted me while I was playing around.

Consider changing your modem number from time to time. A serious hacker would only be slowed down a few hours by this tactic, because that is about how long it would take him to pry your new number out of the phone company. In this instance, though, you're not protecting yourself from hackers, but from people who used to have access to accounts on your computer system. It's a useful precaution: There are cases of people who have been fired, began working for other companies in the same field, and found it possible to call up the old computer at the old number and use their old account. What they do once they get in is anybody's guess.

And while we're on this subject, remember to remove old or otherwise unused accounts. Those people who called their old companies had to have accounts to use, and the odds are that they just used their assigned accounts. In most cases, an account almost never gets removed unless the user requests it. But why should the user request it? He's not going to be using the computer anymore, anyway.

Remember, in Chapter One, when I described how I got my first account by entering LEE as both account and password? Well, the owner of that account had not used it for about seven months, and in the three months that I used Lee's account, I never knew him to use it. And here's something else to note: When the system operator found me, he changed the password. He did not remove the account; he just changed the password.

Consider having a telephone operator answer the phones, and having users request the computer. This is the best way to ensure that a scanning hacker will not run across your system. Hackers who are monitoring their computer's calls out will hang up at the sound of a voice. A computer will hang up at the absence of a carrier signal that indicates it has reached another computer. There can be an added security measure in having users request the computer, if the telephone operator can get to know the key computer users by voice. A good alternative is to have a recording answer, as I mentioned earlier.

Have your modems wait at least two rings before answering. As hackers well know, most modems will pick up the phone somewhere between a half and one ring. If you make sure that the phone rings twice before your modem picks it up, you will fool a scanning hacker about sixty percent of the time. If you make sure your phone rings three to four times before your modem answers, almost any scanning hacker will already have moved on. Some hackers even scan by hand, and these people will almost never wait for the second ring to finish.

Try to limit modem use to the accounts of only those people who actually use it. Most systems allow any account to be used, by default, from any terminal. But in almost every case I know of, fewer than twenty percent of a system's users ever use the phone lines. A more representative figure would probably be three to seven percent. While the number of people using phone lines is very likely to go up rapidly as telecommunications becomes more widespread, people who work with such applications as graphics or word processing usually would not need to use the computer over the phone. There was one case in particular that I feel will clearly show how limiting access to the accounts that need it would solve many problems.

The system involved was a powerful mainframe computer. Almost all of the accounts on the system were owned by people who entered text and data, but a few of the accounts were owned by people who used the computer to look things up from a remote location. Because of these few people, there were four or five phone lines going to the computer. Some hackers found the phone lines and, using sophisticated level-three hacking tactics, came up with a word processor's account. After getting onto the system, the hackers were able to obtain several more accounts. Each of these accounts was owned by someone who never used the phone lines, but each of them was still accessible to anyone with a modem, a microcomputer, and a little knowledge about telecommunications. Furthermore, because the account owners never used the phones, they had chosen passwords that were relatively easy to crack. People who actually do use phone lines have a bit more respect for password choice, because they see how available the system is to outsiders.

Be certain your system logs off users who may hang up the phone without logging off properly. This caution doesn't apply to many systems anymore, but hackers learn at the beginning of their "careers" that there will always be a few systems that don't automatically log off forgetful users. This type of gap in your security could allow hackers to set up decoy programs as I discussed in Chapter Five, but more importantly, a hacker could call up on a Friday evening – when the legitimate users are looking forward to the weekend and are the most likely to forget about logging off. In this case, he will not even need a password to use the system, and he will be able to use it on the two days everyone else is gone. It clearly pays to make sure your system logs people off when they hang up.

When a user wants access to your system, he or she must first log on. Since hackers must also log on, it is useful to set up a few barriers to discourage hackers who have gotten through to your phone lines and are trying to log on.

LOGGING ON

If possible, remove any type-ahead (character-storage) memory buffers your system may have for storing keystrokes typed in during the log-on phase. When a hacker tries to log onto your system, he is likely to have a hack-hack program already set up for use with his personal computer. This program will throw out an account, a carriage return, a password attempt, another carriage return, and then cycle back to the account for a new password attempt. The program runs very quickly. Before the computer under attack has even had time to check whether the account/password combination is valid, the hacker's program has already sent the next password attempt.

Because of this speed, the hacker must depend on the fact that the host computer has a buffer for temporary storage of characters that come in too fast for immediate processing. If there is no such buffer, the hacker will either need to write a special program for your system or he will have to alter one he wrote for another computer. Most hackers wouldn't bother; if your system has no type-ahead buffer for log-on attempts, they'll switch to another tactic or simply try another computer.

Make sure your system hangs up after one or two incorrect attempts to log on. Very few users, especially if they were aware of security risks, would complain bitterly about having only one or two attempts to get their account and password right. Many systems are already using this technique, and I'm sure hackers will learn to live with the slight inconvenience when it's a bit more common. But for the moment, hackers would rather choose an easier target that doesn't hang up so often, or that doesn't hang up at all. It takes time to call a computer back for every log-on attempt.

Consider having your system cut off all incoming modem calls if anyone makes five to ten unsuccessful log-on attempts in a row. The system could allow the users who were currently working with it to remain on, but after five to ten unsuccessful tries, your modems would refuse to answer any more incoming calls. The system operator could then reset the lines anywhere from two minutes to an hour later.

If this system of security were adopted by a computer system, a hacker would assume that these people must have a lot to protect, and thus, thinking security is too tight, would move on to an easier system. The main problem with this security measure is that, once it becomes more well known, it could be used by crashers to keep users from calling in. I have only encountered one computer system that used this method, and it seemed to work, but I still think the situation is tailor-made for a crasher: All he has to do is keep calling with unsuccessful log-on attempts, and no one can use the system.

A slightly better variation of this method would call for turning off only the affected phone line for five to ten minutes. If your other phone lines are well hidden, as I've described in this chapter, they could then remain accessible to your legitimate users.

In any case, this is not a good idea unless you are trying to be very secure.

Let the hacker know you are concerned about security by having the system transmit a reminder before it hangs up. In a few cases, this action would only motivate the hacker. But if the system says something like VALID ACCOUNT NOT GIVEN – NOTIFYING SECURITY OPERA-TOR, the average hacker will figure (probably correctly) that the security on this system is above average. He will then either move on or decide to try and "talk" to the security officer by typing HELLO?? and hitting Control-G (which makes the bell ring) a few times. As long as no operator answers, all will be well. If an operator does answer, well . . . try the approaches discussed in Chapter Eleven.

On a *secure* system, it is worth provoking one or two hackers by reminding them of your security. Most will move on, and that's what you want. On a secure system, you are pretty well protected from hackers getting on, so your concerns are more with keeping them from tying up computer time and phone lines in the first place.

Set a limit to the number of users (two or three is fine) who can use one account at any given time. Almost all computer systems allow many people to log onto the same account at the same time. But at least ninety percent of all users today have no need to use one account at the same time as five or ten other people. Hackers, however, use this feature to make one account work like many: They divide one account into subaccounts for family and friends. There's no point in keeping a vulnerability you don't need in the first place.

Have your system ask the user to verify the last log-on date or time. Most systems do tell users when their accounts were last used, but with the exception of one or two systems, most of those I've seen also allow users to ignore this information altogether–so they normally do. For example, a system that requests verification might show the user something like this:

Account? **SMITH**

Password? **XXXXXX**

Welcome John Smith. You have new mail.

Last Logon Jan. 11, 1985 – – Verify? **Y**

An N response to the verify question should close down the account so that the system operator has to reset it. Make it clear to users that when they verify the last log-on time, they are taking responsibility for any damage that may have been done during that session. Verification of account activity won't keep hackers from getting into your system. Nor will it prevent them from using an account, since all they need do is type Y to keep it open. What verification will do is alert you, the users, and the system operators to hacker activity. And once you know that hackers are on your system, you can take steps to remove or change the account and password or to tighten your system security all around.

Don't give the hacker any information before he's logged on. Your system should not prematurely give out information that is requested by a hacker (or a user). On some systems, for example, typing HELP before logging on will actually get the hacker to the system's help files. In other cases, the request will only tell the hacker the format for account names or, perhaps, the name and phone number of the person to call if you have trouble. By far the worst thing to do, however, is allow hackers to find out who is logged on at the time. Making this information accessible is like handing them all kinds of accounts and asking them to try and get the passwords – and they probably will try.

If possible, you should also hide the make and version of your system. A hacker receives quite a bit of help if your system tells him, MEGACOMPUTER OPERATING SYSTEM, VERSION 18.6.4 before he even has to log on.

Don't give the hacker any power before he is logged on. This is an obvious suggestion, but it is not always followed. If your system allows users to do anything before they are properly logged on, it only helps hackers. In one extreme instance, the Inner Circle was able to find out the password of the last person who logged onto the system, because that system allowed users to examine memory cells without logging on. Granted, examining memory requires some technical ability, but high-level hackers often have both the motivation and the knowledge to do such things.

There is also another, easier, loophole that is still reasonably common. At least one operating system, TOPS, on a DEC-10, lets you type messages to other users without logging on. Thus, a hacker can talk to other users and even set up a remote sysop program if he wants to – all without logging on. This particular system is a little outdated for a corporate computer, but smaller businesses, as well as many schools, are now using it.

Passwords are a basic form of security used by every serious multi-user system. In many cases, passwords are both the system's first and last lines of defense. Judging by my own experiences I would estimate that, if it weren't for password misuse, at least eighty percent of all hackers would never see the inside of a large computer. Here are a few tips on using and assigning passwords.

PASSWORDS

If possible, avoid the use of a single, default password. A default password is one that is given to all accounts when they are first opened. The account owners are then expected to change the default password to a private password of their own choosing. For example, if two different potential users apply for accounts on their company computer, and the computer uses PASS as a default password, both users will be assigned the password PASS.

While they are expected to change passwords, users almost never do. And sooner or later, a hacker finds out about the defaults – more often than not through a contact within the company. Hackers know that defaults are seldom changed. In fact, an international mail company that used default passwords became well known for using the password A for most of its accounts. And, when hackers found out about this, of course they used the information. Once they were on the company's system, a few even managed to get high-level accounts that had no default password. The hackers used these high-level accounts to create their own accounts on the mail system.

Be wary of using a predictable method, or pattern, of assigning passwords. Although a systematic method is a much better way to assign passwords than the default method I just described, many of the "systems" people use are just too simple. I've seen many systems – like the first one I got onto – in which the password is the same as the account name. A few more overly simple patterns that are commonly used are first names, birthdates, and last names. You could probably get away with something like spelling the last name backward for a while, but if a hacker catches on to your system, he will be able to use the information to his advantage as easily as he can any other system. If you must use a systematic method of assigning passwords, make it partly dependent on the date or time the password is issued.

Don't assign long, random passwords. These passwords are almost always hard to remember, so people are either going to change their passwords to a single easily remembered character, or they are going to write down their complicated passwords somewhere. Obviously, secret passwords are not meant to be written down; any time they are, the odds that they will be seen lying on a desk or be found in the trash go up quite a bit.

Another problem with random passwords is that they are often typed slowly – because they are strings of nonsense characters and also because the user doesn't want to make a mistake. Wouldn't most people have trouble remembering, much less typing, a password like GXLWTDPS? A hacker who was watching, however, would have a chance and the motivation to remember where and in what sequence the user has typed on the keyboard. Some hackers would easily be able to copy a user's sequence of keystrokes when they got home to their terminals.

If your method of assigning passwords is not particularly secure and you can't or don't want to change it, then have your system ask for a new password the first time a new user logs on. You may want to consider doing this no matter how well you are handling password assignment, but if your assignment procedure is not a good one, having the system request a new password is a vital step. If you just assume that users are going to change their passwords, you will find out shortly how wrong you are. For instance, I once "acquired" several passwords to a large high-tech firm's mail system. The owners of the accounts I was using had not changed their default passwords and I used the system for over a year before the passwords did change – by order of management. The users had very little to do with it, but if they had changed their passwords when they received their accounts, I might never have seen the inside of that system.

138

Having your system request a new password is a very good security measure, especially if you don't use defaults or easily guessed passwords for new accounts. If you do use easy "first" passwords, it is possible for a high-level hacker to fool your users in the following way. (Bear in mind, though, that this would be quite a sophisticated hacker.) First, he would monitor the system operator's terminal. When he saw that a new account was being created, he would log onto the account ahead of the actual account owner. When the "change password" program requested a new password, he would probably try to change the password to itself – in other words, the hacker would *have* to change the password to satisfy the system, so to avoid arousing suspicion in the user, the hacker would try to tell the computer that the new password was the same as the original. If this tactic worked, he would then run his own program that would simulate the operating system, allow the user to "log on," request (and record) a new password, and then turn the user over to the real system. When the user logged off, the hacker would then log onto the account, change the password as the user had requested it to be changed, and record the new password for his own future use.

Make sure that users on the system know how to change their own passwords. I have talked to users who swore that it was impossible to change their passwords. The fact was, all they had to do was type HELP PASSWORD, HELP SET PASSWORD, or something very similar, and the system would walk them through the procedure. The moral of the story is, if users think that passwords are a sysop-given gift, not to be messed with, they will never change them.

Once they know how to change their passwords, be sure your users think of security, as well as convenience. Most of the passwords on a given system are chosen by users with convenience, not security, in mind. Going on past experience, hackers know that a fairly large number of passwords on a given system will consist of a single character. Just about as many will be the user's first name. And quite a few more will be neither first name nor single character, but still something simple, such as PASSWORD. These users were not thinking of security when they chose their passwords, so those people who do care about security – managers or system operators – must remind them.

There is one other class of users to consider, too: the ones who choose run-of-the-mill passwords, such as SECRET or SEX. In most cases, these users are thinking of security when they choose a password, and perhaps they think they are being quite clever – they just don't realize how many other people think the same thing.

The Best Passwords

The problem of password assignment is not likely to go away anytime soon, unless some radical new development somehow solves the security problem. So how can a single system operator assign four hundred passwords so that each one will be different from the others, yet all of them will be simple enough for the users to remember easily? The problem is solvable in several different ways; the methods differ according to how your system is set up. If the operator is required to enter the password, then, of course, the choice is up to the operator. In most cases, however, the system can be set up to do the work.

The best procedure I have seen for password assignment was a custom software subroutine. The program chose a word at random from a list of over ten thousand five- and six-letter words, and then it added two random characters. The result was an easy-to-remember password, such as RINGER SQ or STICK CJ, that, because of the two meaningless characters, a hacker had little chance of hacking. Even if the hacker could get the data base that contained the words, he would (in theory) still need to go through as many as $10,000 \times 26 \times 26$ possible combinations for each account. Common password procedures that seem to work well include running two words together or allowing the user to choose a very personal password of his or her own and communicating the password verbally to the sysop before the operator creates his or her account.

DISGUISING YOUR SYSTEM

This is a very good time for hackers: They have the luxury of choice. One large network brags of having over twelve hundred systems on it. Another claims over eight hundred. Both networks can be called from most cities with nothing more than a local phone call. These are two examples out of many. With so much to choose from, why, then, would a hacker settle for anything but what he wants? Depending on the hacker, "what he wants" could be as simple as a computer that is on a network and thus is very accessible. For most hackers, however, the ideal is a computer that doesn't make him work too hard to get in. For a few others, it might be the name of a large or famous company, or it could be a very expensive, state-of-the-art computer.

In most cases, though, a simple cosmetic change in your system will make a curious hacker move on in search of what seems to be a more interesting system. Consider these two examples:

M-C   prts inv SYSB

12(7.8)

OP +

Account?

and

MegaCar Corp/Parts inv SYSTEMB

120 Ports (78 logged in)

Operator present

Account?

The first example contains all the information present in the second example but, unless you already know whom you're calling, it hides the fact that a large company owns the system, and that the system itself is fairly large (120 ports). The first example would likely cause many hackers to move on to something they recognized or that sounded more interesting; the second, given the company name and the obvious size of the system, would probably make most hackers sit up and take notice. Both displays would tell an informed user everything he or she needed to know, so the only person who would be "hurt" by the terseness of the first example would be the hacker you want to discourage in the first place.

CHAPTER EIGHT

External Security Devices

Some people believe that security devices like the ones I'll describe in this chapter are the best possible solutions to the problem of computer security. To some extent, they're right. But as you've seen, security depends on people, and the effectiveness of any security device depends not only on the device itself, but on the hacker who is attempting to defeat it and on the other security measures that back up the device. I don't think hardware alone will ever ensure complete security — at least not until it is as "intelligent" as a determined hacker. Still, as I noted in Chapter Six, ninety percent security is all that most systems need. And some of the equipment currently available is very effective, at least as far as deterring most hackers. Or, rather, it's effective as long as the system operator or security manager doesn't fall into the trap of thinking that other security measures, such as password procedures, are rendered obsolete by the fancy new hardware.

Some advertisements claim security systems that are as close to one hundred percent uncrackable as possible. Others boast limitless numbers of security codes, claiming that a hacker would spend hundreds or thousands of years trying to break these codes. If you are thinking about buying one of these devices, ask some questions of yourself and of the equipment vendor before you buy: "How does it work?" "How effective (and cost-effective) is it?" and "Is it what I need?" This chapter will try to answer such questions for most of the equipment now available.

The companies that sell these devices tell you (understandably) every good point about their systems. But since very few things in this world are flawless, I'll point out some of the vulnerabilities of these methods of defense, too – at least as far as hackers are concerned. In addition, because colorful literature sometimes does not explain exactly what the device does, I'll also try to explain how each of these devices works.

Almost every security device now available fits into one of two categories: data encryption or callback. Briefly, data encryption is a method of encoding data so that the information will be unreadable without a code-breaking "key." Callback is a method of limiting access to a computer by having the system verify a user's authorization and then call the user back at a specified phone number. We'll examine these two methods in depth, and then briefly go over the other security fixes that are, or are becoming, available.

ENCRYPTION
DEVICES

By their nature, encryption devices are not intended to keep hackers out of any computer system. Rather than limit access to the machine, they limit access to *information*. They are designed to keep some or all of the data on a system secret by rendering the information unreadable. An encryption device can be either hardware or software. In either case, most such devices take *text* and alter it according to a *key* that is either chosen by the user or is generated as a string of random characters by the device itself. When the information needs to be read, the same process of alteration is applied in reverse.

If the device is hardware-based, the encryption unit is placed between the computer and the terminal. The device does not require a user to run any special encryption program, and it both encrypts

144

outgoing data and decrypts incoming data. With most such hardware encryption devices, the risk of losing or guessing the key is minimal, because the user does not need to choose or keep track of the key. If the device is software-based, the user must run a special program to encrypt or decrypt files. In this case, the program will ask the user for a file and a key, and it will encrypt or decrypt the file using the key given by the user.

How Data Encryption Works

Here is a simplified example of the way encryption works. Let's assume that we have in the computer a small text file we want to have encrypted. We'll name our file SAMPLE and simply let it consist of the phrase OUT OF THE INNER CIRCLE.

Now the fun begins. We run a program called Encrypt, and it asks us what file we would like to encrypt. We respond with SAMPLE, and the program requests a key to use in encrypting it. For this example, we will choose a very simple key, the word *KEY*. The program will then internally match up the key/text combination as follows:

```
K E Y K E Y K E Y K E Y K E Y K E Y K E Y K E Y K E
| | | | | | | | | | | | | | | | | | | | | | | | | | |
O U T   O F   T H E   I N N E R   C I R C L E
```

Next, the program will encrypt the text of our file, using the ASCII system. As you may recall, a standard ASCII character set includes 128 different characters. We call them characters, and so they are to a computer, but not all of them look like ABC's and 123's. Some are what are called control characters that ring bells, symbolize carriage returns, and so on. Regardless, each character is assigned a unique number from 0 to 127.

For our simple example, the program Encrypt will take the ASCII value of the character in the top line and then subtract it from the value of the matching character in the bottom line, "wrapping around" (going back to 127) if the values go below 0. The first O in our text file will be transmitted as the ASCII code for Control-D. The second O in this text, however, will be transmitted as the ASCII code for Control-J. (If you want to follow through on this process, the ASCII codes and the results of this encryption are shown on the next page.)

THE ASCII CODES

0	^@	26	^Z	52	4	78	N	104	h
1	^A	27	^[	53	5	79	O	105	i
2	^B	28	^\	54	6	80	P	106	j
3	^C	29	^]	55	7	81	Q	107	k
4	^D	30	^^	56	8	82	R	108	l
5	^E	31	^_	57	9	83	S	109	m
6	^F	32	Space	58	:	84	T	110	n
7	^G	33	!	59	;	85	U	111	o
8	^H	34	"	60	<	86	V	112	p
9	^I	35	#	61	=	87	W	113	q
10	^J	36	$	62	>	88	X	114	r
11	^K	37	%	63	?	89	Y	115	s
12	^L	38	&	64	@	90	Z	116	t
13	^M	39	'	65	A	91	[	117	u
14	^N	40	(	66	B	92	\	118	v
15	^O	41	)	67	C	93	]	119	w
16	^P	42	*	68	D	94	^	120	x
17	^Q	43	+	69	E	95	_	121	y
18	^R	44	,	70	F	96	`	122	z
19	^S	45	-	71	G	97	a	123	{
20	^T	46	.	72	H	98	b	124		
21	^U	47	/	73	I	99	c	125	}
22	^V	48	0	74	J	100	d	126	~
23	^W	49	1	75	K	101	e	127	Rub Out
24	^X	50	2	76	L	102	f		
25	^Y	51	3	77	M	103	g		

THE ENCRYPTED FILE

O U T   O F   T H E   I N N E R   C I R C L E

K E Y K E Y K E Y K E Y K E Y K E Y K E Y K E

D P { T J 1 T O n y Z o C I k G Z i } M i A @

The underlined characters are control-characters. On a typical terminal, the encoded text file would print out like this:

%{T

    1TnyZoIk <BELL RINGS> Zi}

i

%

And that's it! Pretty unreadable. . . .

When the file is to be decrypted, the program will reverse the process by arranging the text/key combination in the same way and adding the values. This method ensures that each character in the text can be encrypted in many different ways, depending on its position in the text and in relation to the characters in the key. So once you have encrypted the file, it is impossible to read unless it is altered in reverse by the same key and process that altered it in the first place.

More complex methods of encryption use essentially the same technique, but they may go through two or more passes to further encode text, or they may take a simple key, like KEY, and make a longer and more complex key out of it. In addition, hardware encryption devices may use random-number keys that are not chosen by the user and, since they are based on sets of random numbers, cannot, in themselves, be second-guessed by a curious intruder (although the text can *still* be decoded if enough of it follows a known pattern).

Problems with Encryption

One problem with hardware encryption is simply that it's expensive. Most of the time such a device will cost at least $10,000 to install, and it is possible for a hardware encryption setup to cost a lot more.

A second, possibly more important problem that applies to both hardware and software encryption devices is the fact that there will always be the possibility that someone can decode the text. It is true that mathematicians conduct research and publish papers about encryption methods, and encryption standards are closely monitored by the National Security Agency. Even so, you don't have to be in an intelligence agency to crack a code. Standard code-breaking strategies are available in books in any public library. If the encryption method is simple (as in our example) and the person trying to decode your text knows that most of your messages start out...

MEMORANDUM

TO

FROM Bill Landreth

DATE April 1, 1985

SUBJECT

...he or she has plenty of clues to your encryption key in that information alone. Unfortunately, some of the encrypting programs available today are just about that easy to crack or thwart.

You should also be a little wary when you read something like "would take several centuries of computer time to decode your *DATA-SCRAMBLE* encoded text files." The statement is undoubtedly true, but figures of several centuries usually depend on the user entering a complex key that is of a certain length (long), and may contain a few strange characters. Remember from Chapter Five that it would take a hacker twelve-and-a-half thousand years to try every possible upper- and lowercase combination of six letters? Well, some computer systems allow their users to have passwords as long as 256 or 512 characters, including control characters and numerals. If a hacker knew that all passwords on a system were going to be of this type, he would certainly give up. But, of course, people will always pick simpler passwords and keys.

At its core, software encryption, as it is implemented today, is simply a different form of one of the original security concepts: the password. The human factor has always made passwords reasonably easy to guess, so it's not a very good idea to assume that keys will be any more difficult to figure out.

Another possible problem with software encryption devices is that there is no easy way to recover the key if the user were to lose or forget it. After all, if the key could be recovered from the text file, the encryption scheme wouldn't be very good, would it? Because of this risk, even if the user has an excellent memory and chooses a very simple key, he may very well decide to write it down somewhere, "just in case," or even store it in the computer, so that loss of his key won't mean actual loss of the data that he is protecting by having the key in the first place.

Finally, there is a problem associated with some hardware encryption devices that depend either on a special terminal or on a device that is hooked up to a terminal and has the method of decoding text built into it. These devices are vulnerable, because a computer criminal would only need to gain access to the terminal in order to gain access to the computer system.

In theory, callback units are very good ways to keep hackers off a system. Here's basically how they work: When a user calls a computer attached to a callback unit, the callback unit requests the user to enter an ID code. After an ID code is entered, the callback unit hangs up on the user. It then checks the ID code for validity. If the code passes the test, the computer then calls the user back at an authorized phone number it has matched up against the user's ID code. With most callback units, the user then has to go through the normal procedure of entering his account and password. Of course, since the unit verifies the phone number, it will not call a hacker at an unauthorized location. And even if it did, for some reason, the company would have a record of the number it called and would know where to find the hacker.

The better versions of callback units answer the phone and allow the user to enter an ID code only from a touch-tone phone. The computer is not involved in the contact, so there isn't any chance that a hacker could gain access from this point. Less secure callback units, however, have the system answer the call, and they let the caller enter an ID code from his computer.

These latter units offer a hacker a small chance to break out of the controlling program and gain access to the system. The possibility may seem remote, but I have been told that this has been done quite effectively. I heard the story from a system operator on a system that seemed to be very concerned with security. When I asked the operator why it had been so easy for me to get onto their system if they were so worried about security, he told me that they had been rather spoiled by a callback unit. They had depended on this device for several months, but they had to stop using it after it was involved in a major breach of security.

The device that the system had used required that the host computer set up a special account, under which the callback-unit software was run. When a caller called the computer, the main computer, not the callback unit, answered and asked for an ID code. Once the user entered an ID code, the computer searched through its directory of valid codes. If the code was valid, the system hung up and had the modem redial the user. The problem came up if the user happened to hit Control-Z while the system was searching the files.

Control-Z is a common signal used to tell a computer, "That's the end of my file (or input)." When this signal was received by the call-back unit, the result was an "end of file" error. After this error message, the user was no longer under control of the callback program, but in the account set up to be used by the callback-unit software. And from this account, a person could get the entire list of account names and the valid codes and phone numbers of the people authorized to use the system. The company was never able to fix this problem, so it just stopped using the callback device.

Problems with Callback Units

There are a few limitations to the general use of callback modems that you should be aware of before you invest in one.

- ≡ *Unless the company provides specially prepared terminals, the user needs to have some general knowledge of computers, because he or she has to set up a personal computer and modem to answer the main computer's return call.*

- ≡ *The user has to be at a specific, authorized phone number to receive the return call. No calling from a phone booth in Silicon Valley while trying to sell Apples to IBM. Yet this type of accessibility is the reason why many companies need phone lines in the first place.*

- ≡ *Commercial networks are out of the question with callback units. As of right now, I know of no reasonable plan to use a callback unit and a network together.*

- ≡ *The phone call is charged to the main computer. In this age of multiple phone companies and ZUM zoning (a telephone company method of phasing out "local" calls), costs may add up quickly for the computer owner.*

Unlike data encryption devices, callback units are meant to keep unauthorized people out of your system. For the most part, a callback unit does a very good job of stopping the type of hackers I am discussing in this book, but most of these hackers could be stopped just as easily by proper use of passwords. Only you can decide if the extra expense of a callback unit is worth keeping out casual hackers. Bear in mind that a hacker who is also a thief or has other strong motives for getting into your particular system could get around a callback unit in many ways.

Holding the Line

With most phone systems, it is quite possible for the hacker to use the following steps to get around a callback unit that uses the same phone line for both incoming and outgoing calls: First, he calls the callback unit and enters any authorized ID code (this is not hard to get, as you'll see in a moment). After he enters this ID, the hacker holds the phone line open – he does not hang up. When the callback unit picks up the phone to call the user back, the hacker is there, waiting to meet it.

The ID code, as I said, is simple for a hacker to obtain, because these codes are not meant to be security precautions. The callback unit itself provides security by keeping incoming calls from reaching the computer. The ID codes are no more private than most telephone numbers. Some callback units refer to the codes as "location identification numbers," and some locations are used by several different people, so their IDs are fairly well known. I've been told that, in some cases, callback units also have certain simple codes that are always defined by default.

Once the hacker has entered an ID code and the callback unit has picked up the phone to re-call him, the hacker may or may not decide to provide a dial tone to allow the unit to "think" it is calling the correct number. In any event, the hacker will then turn on his computer, connect with the system – and away he goes.

If, however, the hacker has trouble holding the line with this method, he has an option: the intercept.

The Intercept

Holding the line will only work with callback units that use the same phone lines to call in and to call out. Some callback units use different incoming and outgoing lines, but there is an equally simple way to fool them. These systems work like any other callback units, except that, for example, numbers 555-3820 through 555-3830 are dedicated to users' incoming calls, and lines 555-2020 through 555-2030 are dedicated to the computer's outgoing calls.

The only thing a hacker needs in order to get through to these systems is a computer and a little time – he doesn't even need an ID code. First, the hacker calls any one of the outgoing phone lines, which, of course, will not answer. Sooner or later, though, while the hacker has his computer waiting there, listening to the ring, an authorized user will call one of the incoming lines and request to be called back. It will usually be less than an hour's wait, but the hacker's computer is perfectly capable of waiting for days, if need be.

The callback unit will take the code of the authorized user, hang up, verify the code, and pick up the phone line to call back. If the unit tries to call out on the line the hacker has dialed, the hacker has his computer play a tone that sounds just like a dial tone. The computer will then dial the number given that matches up with the user's authorization ID. After that, the hacker can just connect his computer as he would in any other case. If he is really serious, he will even decode the touch tones that the mainframe dialed, figure out the phone number of the user the system was calling, call this person, and make a few strange noises that sound as though the computer called back but didn't work for some reason.

Call Forwarding

Many switching systems around today enable a hacker to use call forwarding to his advantage. If the hacker knows the area code and phone number of an authorized user, he can simply use his contacts within the phone company (something hackers usually have no lack of, thanks to the phone phreaks of the '70s) to set call forwarding on the user's line. Then, the hacker has the user's phone calls forwarded to a place he chooses.

Call forwarding can be used with callback units, and has been used in this way by one thief who worked in the company he robbed. Because he was an employee, he found it easy to get the inside information he needed to have call forwarding set on a friend (and coworker's) house phone. He then used his friend's account to set up a scheme to defraud his company out of nearly one million dollars in technical equipment. The company's managers spent several days working to build a case against the friend, whom the callback modem called, because they believed there was no possible way anyone else could be receiving the computer's return calls. By the time they realized they were wrong, the real thief was long gone.

I haven't heard of this happening, but I think it is possible that a callback modem could have a trapdoor built into it. Callback modems are run by software, which is written by programmers. An unscrupulous programmer could find it very easy to slip in an unpublicized routine, such as, "if code = *43*, then show all valid codes and phone numbers." And such a routine, of course, would leave security wide open to anyone who found the trapdoor. The obvious protection here, assuming the situation ever arises, is simply an ethical manufacturer that checks its software thoroughly before releasing it.

Trapdoors as a Possibility

Callback units don't solve such problems as direct wiretaps or the hacker who is an employee of the company. It's even possible that a burglar or a hacker who is a friend of an employee could call from an employee's house and cause trouble. This vulnerability means that callback units can, in many cases, turn out to be too much trouble and expense for companies guarding against hackers, but not adequate enough, by themselves, for companies guarding against thieves.

Criminals

Encryption and callback technology cover most of the external security devices available today. There are a few others, however, that you can also consider.

OTHER SECURITY DEVICES

With a filter system, a non-computer tone or perhaps a computerized voice answers the phone. The user is then expected to enter an identification number from a touch-tone phone. Once this is done, the filter system hands the caller over to the operating system.

Filter Systems

Filter systems are a kind of compromise between having a callback unit and not having a callback unit. In fact, many callback units can optionally be used as filters—although, if you use a callback unit as a filter, you are also paying extra for features that you don't use.

As a security measure, filter systems are good for guarding against casual hackers, primarily because the price is usually lower than that of most callback units, with about the same effectiveness against all but the most dedicated hackers. Most filter systems also notify the operator if there are more than a certain number of incorrect attempts at an identification number – a good idea, because hackers might otherwise decide to leave an autodialer on the system for a few hours. On the other hand ... a filter system with a 90-decibel alarm that the operators can't shut off might only make it more fun for a Crasher to put an autodialer on the system.

Improved Log Systems

Almost every computer system has a program, a user log, that is always running and is supposed to keep track of users. But there are different types of user logs. Some only contain information that looks like this:

Account STD123 logged in at 7:48:7 for 55 minutes and 1 second.

This user log just tells who logged on, when, and for how long. A user log may, however, contain information that looks like this:

Account STD123 logged in at port 061 with modem 9 at 7:48:7 for 55:01.

Account accessed: Home directory at 7:49:16, Account directory at 8:10:38, System directory at 8:11:2, Home directory at 8:20:21.

Account sent mail to user(s) STD33, STD768.

Account had total of 6 errors and 1 help access.

This log tries to follow the user through the system. First, it tells us the user called and used port 61, modem 9. This person first used his or her assigned directory – the *Home* directory. Then, the user went over to the *Account* and *System* directories, and nine minutes later went back to the *Home* directory. Sometime during the log-on period, the user made six errors, asked for help once, and "mailed" two electronic letters.

More secure systems – those that would not even allow a phone line within fifty yards of the computer installation – might have user logs that actually record every single keystroke a user enters. At the other end of the spectrum, the least secure systems may not have user-log systems at all. But most systems fall somewhere in between these extremes, and I know of one, a mainframe computer, running a custom-made operating system for a large real-estate company, that came close to hitting both extremes in a matter of a few days.

The operators on this system normally never bothered to keep logs – they felt the computer time saved in not running the log program was more than enough compensation for the security risk involved. One slow day they were bored, so they offhandedly decided to run their log program to see what was going on in the system.

Their log program kept simple records, like the first of the two preceding examples, but the one thing that stood out was the fact that one account seemed to be in constant use. The operators did not recognize the account, and wondered why it seemed to be active for at least six of the seven hours they had run their log program. So, they decided to write their own program, one that would record more accurately what the account was doing and what type of files it was keeping. What they found surprised them.

They had expected to find some program that would notify a realtor if a house came along with more than X square feet, at a price of less than Y dollars. What they actually found was a bulletin-board system set up by hackers. After reading the messages on the bulletin board – which had been there for eight months – the operators posted this message of their own:

> From now on, this bulletin board system will not allow access
> between the hours of 11:00 AM and 3:00 PM due to excessive
> demands on the system during this time.
>
> Users of this system will also be expected to continue their
> practice of non-destructiveness.
>
> Thank You,
>
> Your new Sysops.

Companies that sell improved user logs, which may be in the form of either hardware or software, claim that the device will make it easier

Problems and Solutions

to tell who logged on, what they did while they were on, and when they logged off. Quite often, a system that is supposed to improve the system logs is included with a callback unit or other security device. The problem with any software, and some hardware, log system is that the more accurate the log, the more computer time is spent keeping it. Some systems are already overworked and can't even run the log that originally came with the machine, much less a more elaborate one.

In addition, system logs are generally ignored by system operators, and in most cases it is hard to blame them. A very good log on a busy system might produce, on a daily basis, a hundred pages of user information for the operators to look over. A very poor log system might only produce one page of information, but it also might not have a chance of showing a hacker's activity. With either type of log, even if the operator spends an hour every day checking the system logs, he might not find anything wrong for years. Besides, an operator who has spent an hour a day looking over the logs may start to get lazy after three years. Then, if he "forgets" to read over the system log every day, his manager, in turn, may think that the system is secure because nothing is reported wrong with the logs. Often, operators compromise by ignoring the logs and simply watching activity on the system from time to time.

An improved log system would make life easier for the operator and harder for the hacker. A perfect user-log system would automatically notice strange activities and record this information in a way that would make it easy for the operator to see among the rest of the (mostly useless) data: bold-faced print, perhaps, or a different color, or underlining. Things an improved log system *should* detect include more than two users on one account, more than one false attempt on a valid account's password, access to system files (files used by the system, but not to be used by users), and too many help-file accesses (a favorite ploy of hackers).

Terminals with
Unique IDs

This type of system is very secure if it is set up and used right, but it can also be the most costly to implement. It involves using special terminals, each of which has a different ID code. The system to which the terminals are connected requests each terminal's ID code every now and then when the terminal is in use. Less secure systems like this will ask only once, but the more secure systems may be asking constantly. In a properly arranged setup of this sort, the system asks the terminal for its ID in thousands of different ways. In English, these questions are along the lines of:

"Give me your ID."

"May I have your ID?"

"Who are you?"

"Tell me your ID number."

...and so on, for several thousand different variations of the same question. The terminal itself has thousands of answers to return – one unique answer for every one of these unique questions. If the terminal gets any of the answers wrong, the computer will ask a few more times and then refuse to talk to the terminal anymore.

This type of security measure is best suited for terminals that are not to be used over the phone system, because the extra communications needed for ID questions and answers would slow down communications too much. Telephone communication, remember, is much slower than computer-to-computer or computer-to-terminal communication. Besides, at this high level of security, your concern is more likely to be theft or espionage, rather than hacking, and encryption solves phone-related security risks better. If you need this level of protection, you may need something better than an ID system.

Nonstandard Devices

I have encountered modems that operate at 500, 600, and 1800 baud (rather than the usual 300 and 1200 baud); terminals that use a personalized character set, rather than ASCII; and computers that require the user to type the Delete character as enter and the Enter key as delete. In the installations I have seen, all of these nonstandard methods were very effective in keeping hackers out because, as I've said before, it's best from the hacker's point of view to move on to easier systems to crack. Computer criminals would have little problem getting around this type of system if it used a nonstandard method alone, but for keeping thieves out, I would bet on a system that had educated users, nonstandard baud rates, educated users, a callback system, excellent logs with careful personnel to watch them, educated users, and a good encryption device.

Not many systems use nonstandard equipment, so my experience with them is limited, but I would say that if you want to keep out casual hackers, you would do well to look into this idea.

A company must still provide terminals that are capable of using nonstandard signals, but part of the reason nonstandard devices are worth looking into is the fact that using them may be no more expensive than using standard equipment, and may be as effective at keeping out casual hackers as a $20,000 encryption system.

THE
FUTURE

Data security can only improve. The computer-security industry will mature as companies that produce security devices revise their products and work on resolving complaints from customers. Ultimately, companies will come up with better encryption, callback, and password-protection schemes. System programmers are spending more effort in preserving security. And as for the computers themselves, consider that most of the machines built before 1980 essentially had no built-in security when compared to those being built today.

Once user education is accepted as a vital part of computer security and corporate executives know how to choose the security measures best suited for their system, unauthorized computer trespassing will take a giant step backward. But if better security is inevitable, advances in technology and security enhancement are open to our imagination.

Passphrases

I don't know when the changeover will happen, but I think the computer community is not far from abandoning passwords in favor of passphrases. A passphrase like THE CAT JUMPED QUICKLY will be much easier to remember and assign, as well as much harder for the intruder to guess. Of course there will always be a few passphrases that hackers will be able to use successfully – predictable ones, like I AM JOHN, LET ME IN, or I LOVE YOU. But all things considered, widespread use of passphrases will definitely be a security boon.

158

This technique seems to be a natural method for use with telecommunications, because the medium of identification, the voice, is easily sent over phone lines. Computer-based systems for identifying voices have been under development for a long time, and voice-recognition technology is reportedly on the verge of reaching a widely acceptable level. A system using voice verification would probably answer with a tone, have the user key in an ID number, and then ask the user to state his or her full name. Unless the person were to key in the correct number and pass the voice test, no computer contact would be made. If the caller did pass both tests, the computer could make the connection or a callback process could start. And for additional security, the user could just enter an account and password as usual, before being allowed access to any files.

Voice Verification

Fingerprint verification is now used only in some of the most sensitive computer systems in the world, but assuming that the speed of technology follows the pattern it has set in the past, more systems will be able to afford fingerprint verification in the future. The units in use today are already quite accurate, but no doubt these systems will become more and more accurate. Because of the element it checks, this is one system of verification that will probably not apply to mainstream telecommunications for quite a while.

Fingerprint Verification

Signature-verification techniques as a security measure seem to be very promising, although they, too, probably will not be used with telecommunications security for quite a while, if ever. Current systems in use allow a person to enter an account name and then provide a signature. The computer checks not only the look of the signature, but also the amount of pressure applied and the speed used to sign the name. Studies show that, because of the uniqueness and number of these identifying features, even an accomplished forger can't fool the computer.

Signature Verification

Computer security is a matter of balance. If every house, bank, candy store, or used-car lot were as secure as Fort Knox, life wouldn't be very

KEEPING THE BALANCE

easy. The same consideration applies to security devices. Each one could, by itself, eliminate most of the security problems that are likely to be encountered by most computer systems – but you have to use any device correctly, and as it applies to your system and your needs.

A company that has not even used its password system adequately would probably find it a waste to move up to another system of protection.

You have to pay heed to all aspects of security, and all aspects of your security requirements, very carefully before investing in any security device. In terms of making a choice, you should also pay close attention to all aspects of the device itself. One program I ran across that was operating under the Primos operating system shows a good example of placing too much emphasis on colorful advertisements and too little on critical evaluation of the product.

The programmer on the system involved was interested in an addition to the operating system that allowed him to set up password protection on all files. Before anyone tried to run, read, erase, or otherwise alter a file, that person would have to enter a password. This system, said the advertisement, would provide a second level of password protection. The security vendor even made sure to tell the system programmer to choose good passwords when locking up the files that controlled the system.

This all sounds like a good idea, and it is. But the programmer did not question the software patch enough before telling the company that owned the computer to buy the addition. The software was set up in such a way that it allowed anyone to obtain a printout of the entire password file with one simple command.

Caveat emptor. It's a caution that applies to computers as well as cars – especially since high technology implies a high degree of complexity and requires a certain amount of background knowledge.

CHAPTER NINE

Microcomputers and Security

ackers have a wide range of *interesting* machines to play with–on any given day, an average hacker probably has access to over a million dollars in computer equipment. Why, then, a chapter on security and microcomputers? I can think of two good reasons: First, with more and more people using micros every day, it is becoming more important for users of these machines to think about the security of microcomputer data and programs. Second, just because hackers are not beating on the doors of your disk drive does not mean you are immune to the need for security precautions. There are, indeed, instances in which hackers can become interested in microcomputers (though perhaps these instances are more recreational than professional), and there are instances in which a thief or some other intruder might find an office microcomputer quite fascinating.

Three categories of people need to worry about security when dealing with microcomputers: people who use microcomputers to access larger systems, those who use microcomputers in their business, and those who use microcomputers to run bulletin-board systems. This chapter will look at the security needs of these types of users.

USING A MICRO WITH OTHER SYSTEMS

If you are like most people who use mainframes from a remote location, you use a microcomputer and a modem. A microcomputer used as a smart terminal can do a very good job of helping you work with larger systems, and it can provide much more power than a dumb terminal. A microcomputer can save data sent from the mainframe to the user; it can dial the computer and log the user on automatically; it can transmit files from the user to the mainframe; and it can be made to emulate different types of dumb terminals when necessary.

The only problem with using a microcomputer to access other systems is that, as you will see in the following section, you can find yourself "done in" by the same sophistication that makes your micro so easy to use.

Autologon Macros

Autologon macro is computer jargon for a type of computer short-hand. Although it may sound technical, the term simply refers to an AUTOmatic LOGON procedure that is stored as a MACRO which, in turn, is simply a long sequence of keystrokes (commands) represented and activated by, usually, a single keystroke.

Telecommunications software and other microcomputer programs often enable users to store long strings of often-used commands as one or a few keystrokes. For example, with one common type of autologon macro, you simply tell your personal computer the system you want to call by entering its name. The macro then has your computer dial the number, connect with the system, and enter your account name and/or password. It may even check your mail and log you off automatically. Autologon macros can be a great help, and I use them whenever possible. Macros save a great deal of time and effort, but they can also be a security risk.

The first and most common risk with these macros stems from the fact that microcomputer owners frequently trade software. Suppose, for example, you use macros for telecommunications with a computer on a network, such as THE SOURCE, or maybe with the secure computer back in the home office. You've told a friend how great your communications software is, and one day you copy the disk for your friend to try. This is someone you trust, so you hand over the disk without thinking anything of it. Think again. Your macros are stored on that disk – phone numbers, account names, passwords. Of course you can trust your friend, but what if your friend trades the disk, just as you did? I have received terminal programs that have moved through thousands of miles and at least ten people before they reached me. And when they did get to me, they included secret account and password information that had not yet been discovered or used by other hackers.

Another problem with autologon macros is that hackers have been known to be able to activate them from a remote location, either via a bulletin board or over a mainframe. A hacker who ran a bulletin-board system would be able to tell the smart terminal (by sending the correct sequence of characters) to show him all the macros.

Bulletin Boards

If you use a microcomputer for telecommunications and are an active member of the bulletin-board community, there is another potential risk you can eliminate with a little precaution: password security.

People who call bulletin boards usually have at least two or three passwords to remember – bulletin-board passwords, mainframe passwords, network passwords. With several to many passwords to keep track of, it is very tempting to use one common password for all of your accounts – both bulletin-board and mainframe. Many people, in fact, do use the same passwords, even if they have only two or three to remember. Hackers are well aware of this, and bulletin-board owners are often sympathetic to hackers, so be careful. There's no point in using a private password to a secure system as a bulletin-board password on a much less secure, much more public, system.

MICROS IN
SMALL
BUSINESSES

A business microcomputer poses its own types of security problems. Because very few are even hooked up to the phone system, and almost none are hooked up to networks, hackers very rarely try to get into a business microcomputer. This same computer, however, may well be open to theft of programs or data; so there are many aspects to micro-computer security in this area, as well.

Micros and Hackers

The overwhelming majority of people who are qualified to work with microcomputers are not active hackers, but hackers do get jobs work-ing with computers, because they are generally well qualified by nature and, well, inclination for the work. If you gave such a hacker free access to your system, he might be unable to resist the oppor-tunity and decide to do some of his "work" from your computer and modem. If you didn't have a modem, he might provide his own with-out bothering to tell you about it. His hacking would probably involve setting up a program to scan phone numbers overnight or to execute a hack-hack on some large system.

In any case, the hacker may not be as careful as he would be at home, and if a legal problem happened to result, then you, as the owner of the computer, could be held responsible. You should consult an attorney for all the ins and outs in this rapidly changing area of the law, but on a day-to-day basis, there are two precautions you can use to try and avoid this problem in the first place: Limit use of the micro-computer and modem to certain people by using some type of lock and key, or familiarize yourself with the work being done on the com-puter and watch the people using the computer so that you can spot unusual activities quickly.

Micros and Passwords

Microcomputers are well known for their lack of security, but in most cases, since these are single-user systems, these computers don't need better security. There are cases, however, in which an operating sys-tem for a micro or a minicomputer has a password feature that is spotlighted as a major security device but is one that turns out to be very easily defeated. In some instances, if the hacker removes a floppy disk at just the right moment, he can get around the password feature altogether. In others, he may find it possible to read the password files themselves, no tricks involved. It is more likely, though, that any of the techniques explained in Chapter Five would be much more effec-tive and easy to use on most micros than on even the least secure mainframe.

It doesn't take anyone long to walk up to a microcomputer and copy a file or two over to a pre-formatted disk. It is even easier if the person works in the organization and doesn't have to look out of place. Because of this, a thief would find it much less difficult to go after a business with floppies he can access than a mainframe he would have to call. With microcomputers handling so many jobs these days, a business that keeps any type of secret data on a microcomputer has to be very careful in this regard.

A thief could, for example, copy the data to his own floppy disk, change it in a way that helped him, and replace the altered floppy. Or, he could just take the floppy and use the data to his own or a competing company's advantage. Whatever he might decide to do with the data, one point is clear: The fact that users of the microcomputer have no idea of what's going on makes it easy to take or copy floppy disks. If the users were more aware, the thief would have as much trouble taking a floppy disk as he would taking a thousand-dollar bill.

Here are a few tips to keep in mind when managing a micro with floppy drives.

Educate users. At the risk of sounding like a bore, I'll stress this point again. User education is the most important aspect of computer security. I would guess that at least 90 percent of all computer crime depends on the unwilling aid of people who don't know what they are doing. And wherever there are confused people, there are other people waiting to profit from their confusion.

Keep floppies under lock and key. Some owners of business micro- and minicomputers keep a lock on the disk-drive door. This is a good idea, but it is also important to have the floppy contents of the drive locked away when they are not in use. And perhaps the most important thing to remember is: Keep the backups as secure as you keep the originals. It's funny, but some people guard their original disks as closely as they can, but they leave their backups lying around like dead leaves. I suppose there's something very human in thinking that a copy is a copy. . . is not an original. But we're talking about computer data, not Rembrandts. To a computer, a copy is a copy *is* an original, and the moral is: Only the people who need to use any floppies need to have the key to access them.

FLOPPY DISKS AND SECURITY

Keep inventory. This precaution is so that you will know if one of your disks is missing. An inventory can be your microcomputer equivalent of a mainframe user log, and if you keep records of who used which disk, when, and for what job, it may also help you to find out who took a disk without authorization, because you will have a good idea of when it was taken and who had access to it at that time. Once again, remember to treat backup disks or tapes as carefully as you do your originals.

Data encryption. There are quite a few data-encryption software packages available for microcomputers, and in many ways they could solve the security problems facing microcomputer owners. If all data were encrypted as it was saved, and then decrypted as it was read, all data on any disk would be unreadable and unchangeable to a thief.

There are a few pitfalls involved with data encryption, however. First, the key has to be closely guarded against both loss and discovery. A lost key could mean lost data because the key is not saved on disk with the data, as a password is. In the worst case, suppose that the only person who knew the key died. That data could be lost forever. On the other hand, loss could also mean loss of data in the sense of an employee who leaves your company on less than friendly terms – with the key memorized – and goes to work for your biggest competitor.

Another pitfall is one that encryption has in common with passwords: People choose keys that they can remember, and that hackers can often guess.

Be conscientious about keeping backups. I don't mean just backups on disks or tape. Of course you need these, but you should always have some kind of written record of all the transactions you make. The computer has not yet replaced paper and ink; it has only made paper and ink easier to deal with. Information stored on magnetic media is very volatile and easy for someone to destroy.

Once again, you have to treat *all* your floppies as if they were original data. In some cases, a thief will find it impossible to get to original floppy disks, but he can quite easily get to the backups. As I said earlier, he could then do one of two things, depending on his motives. He might create and alter a new backup in his favor and damage the data disk being used (with a magnet, perhaps, or power surges or one of many other physical attacks). The company would find that its data disk is damaged and be forced to use the altered backup. On the other hand, of course, a thief could just back up the backup, take one,...and no one would be the wiser.

At this time, small businesses that use microcomputers seem to have more trouble finding employees to run computers than they do deciding on and buying the machines themselves. After spending $15,000 on a computer system and wondering what to do with it, they have been forced to hire one person who "seems to know what he's talking about." What follows is one person telling twenty other people how to use the computer system.

Employee Risks

In many cases, a situation like this will tempt the one person who knows what he's doing to use the system to his own advantage: keep personal records on the system, or print personal letters. After all, there's no harm being done. In other cases, the person who knows what he's doing might find it very simple to print more paychecks for himself or to have his expense-account check automatically padded every month. This kind of crime is known to experts as "data diddling," and it is different from the "pure" variety of hacking that's primarily the subject of this book. Still, since there is no one to check on these "diddles," they could go on for a long time without being discovered. In fact, they have – with and without computers – for as long as *embezzlement* has been a definable word.

Another thing that this type of "expert" employee usually turns out to be good at is writing software for the employer. It would be a very simple matter, however, for such an employee to throw a trapdoor or two into his other programs – some software authors would. In most cases the trapdoor would just be a little secret, not meant to cause any harm, but put there for fun by the author. It could be, however, that the author puts in a trapdoor so that he will always have access to the accounting programs, or so that he can access the payroll program whenever he wants to find out who is getting paid what. In any case, once trapdoors are in your system, they can be almost impossible to find without hundreds of hours of detective work by a skilled and thorough computer professional.

BULLETIN
BOARDS

Now we have come to the "recreational" side of hacking and micro-computers. Aside from such matters as password security, which was discussed earlier, most business users will probably have little direct interest in bulletin boards – their attraction is mainly social or professional, rather than business related. Still, hackers use bulletin boards for two interesting reasons: one, to communicate what they know, and two, to crash the system and thus irritate a lot of people at once. The first reason is more important to you as a user, owner, or operator of a large computer. The second is, well, interesting for its own sake.

In order to understand how bulletin boards are used (and mis-used), you need to understand what they are and what they do. First, we'll look briefly at the ways bulletin boards are set up, used, and maintained. Then, for those of you who have never seen a bulletin board, I'll show you two samples – one public and freely accessed by anyone, and one private and for hackers' use only.

*Bulletin Boards
In General*

A bulletin-board system, often abbreviated to BBS, is usually a personal computer equipped with a modem and special software that allows people to call in and use the system. Often, the bulletin board is set up and left permanently running as an open forum for anyone who feels like calling in. In other cases, the bulletin board is open during certain specified hours. In any event, a bulletin board is almost always set up as a free service by a special-interest group that simply wants to make such a system available to others.

A microcomputer – or any computer, for that matter – becomes a bulletin-board system by virtue of its special program, which allows the computer and modem to "listen" to a telephone line for a phone call. Whenever an outside computer equipped with a modem calls the telephone number of the bulletin-board computer, the BBS software allows the host system to record input from the remote computer. In many cases, the software can also transmit text or even programs to the remote computer. BBS software is also responsible for keeping track of messages that various users place on the bulletin board, and most bulletin-board software offers options for both public and private messages – users can send private mail to one another or they can post public messages for everyone to read.

168

When people call bulletin-board systems, they are usually asked to enter their names and/or some type of password for identification. Since bulletin boards almost never charge for their services, this password feature is designed to give the system operator some control over who can and who cannot use the bulletin board. In every case I have seen, this decision is made quite fairly. Only those very few people who cause too much trouble by leaving tasteless messages or by trying to crash the board are ever removed from the system. In those instances, the operator denies access to the trouble-maker by eliminating the individual's password from the list of valid entries stored in the bulletin-board computer.

What do people leave messages about? Well, different bulletin boards have different types of users and, therefore, different types of messages. A majority of bulletin boards are meant to be as public as possible, and list such diverse messages as "1978 Ford for sale" and "Summer work wanted." Some boards are dedicated to certain groups of people. There are boards for people who want to discuss religion, and boards for people who want to discuss making money. There are bulletin boards for software pirates, school teachers, hackers, system operators of bulletin boards, single people interested in finding dates, people who like to tell dirty jokes...and even boards for people interested in computers.

When people call a public BBS, the following sample shows the types of messages they will see.

A Public BBS

Welcome to the PCD Bulletin Board system
Please Login or enter "N" if a new user:

X7TLO

The user's ID/password. The system welcomes him by name and tells him he has mail. The user decides to read it. . . .

Welcome Bill. It has been 3 days since
you last logged on. You have new mail.

Read it now?   **Yes**

He is told who sent the mail, when it was sent, and what it's about. . . .

From: Bryan Brown   On: 12/14/84
Subject: Mail
Bill,
    You must have forgotten that I exist.
It has been several weeks since you have
left me any mail. Did you ever get Jim's
phone number from Eric?
Don't forget to answer,

                              Bryan

The user is given a list of choices and decides to answer the letter. . . .

Save, Delete, Re-read, or Answer?   **Answer**

The system tells him what to do. The system will address the message for him, so he only needs to type the message itself. . . .

Enter text now, 50 lines max. Hit
Control-Z to send, Control-C for menu.

Bryan,
   Sorry, you must be talking to the
wrong guy. I don't think I know you.

                         Bill

He hits Control-C (ˆC) to see the menu and chooses to send his letter. . . .

   ˆC
Send, Read, Edit, Add, or Abort?   **Send**

The user is shown another menu. He decides to delete Bryan's message, and tells the system he doesn't want to send any more mail. . . .

Save, Delete, Re-read?   **Delete**
Send any more mail?   **No**

Now, the system puts the user in the main part of the bulletin board. He is once again given a menu to choose from. . . .

MENU OF FUNCTIONS
= – = – = – = – = – = – = – = – = – = – = – =
A:: Tips for Apple Owners
C:: Call Sysop for Chat
E :: Enter Electronic mail section
F :: Leave Feedback for Sysop to read
I :: Tips for IBM Owners
K:: Kill a message
O:: Off -- Hang up
P :: Post Message on Public Board
S :: Scan or Read Public Messages
T :: Tips for TRS-80 Owners
U:: List of Users on the PCD BBS
X:: Turn Expert mode ON

*He is experienced with this bulletin board, so he turns expert mode
on to get rid of the menus....*

Enter Option: **X**

*The system responds and asks what he would like to do next. He
decides to scan/read the public messages....*

Expert mode now >ON<
Option: **S**

*He requests a list of messages, starting with number 25. The system
shows him the number, topic, and writer's name for each one....*

There are 31 messages.
Start at message #:   **25**
25 : Double Siders Jim Elits
26 : X-rays Steve Burlap
27 : I Did! Dan Gaylord
28 : Movies Mort Smith
29 : A Boat Ride Peter Zen
30 : I Resent That! Peter Rollouts
31 : Hello? Kerry McFarl

He decides to start reading at message #26....

Number to read or "Q" to quit?:   **26**

Message 26 Posted on 12-12-84
Re: X-rays By Steve Burlap
  Is it true that if you place your cat
next to your monitor you can see right
through it? I hear that albino cats
work best.
  End of message #26

He decides to read the next one....

Number to read or "Q" to quit?:   **27**

Message 27 Posted on 12-12-84
Re: I Did! By Dan Gaylord
  I tried it once, but a knife works just
as well and is cheaper.
                              Dan
  End of message #27

A response to a previous message.
Once again, he reads the next message....

Number to read or "Q" to quit?:   **28**

Message 28 Posted on 12-13-84
Re: Movies By Mort Smith
  Has anyone seen any good movies lately?
How about "Godzilla Meets The City
Slicker"? is that any good?
  Why don't you guys keep me posted
on movies anymore?
  End of message #28

And the next....

Number to read or "Q" to quit?:   **29**

Message 29 Posted on 12-13-84
Re: A Boat Ride By Peter Zen
  I saw "Godzilla Meets The City Slicker"

and thought it was okay, as far as movies
from Taiwan go. They have no imagination.
   End of message #29

the next. . . .

        Number to read or "Q" to quit?:   **30**

Message 30 Posted on 12-13-84
Re: I Resent That! By Peter Rollouts
   I have a friend from Taiwan (his
name is chuck) and he seems to have a lot
of imagination. He poured red paint over
his older brother's head!
   End of message #30

and the last. . . .

        Number to read or "Q" to quit?:   **31**

*There are always a few new people on the boards. But
they get the hang of it soon. . . .*

Message 31 Posted on 12-13-84
Re: Hello? By Kerry McFarl
   Does this thing work? Can anyone read
this? Damn.
EXIT
FINISHED
HELP
   End of message #31

*Now that he has read all the new messages, he quits and chooses
a new option, P, so he can post a message of his own. . . .*

Number to read or "Q" to quit?: **Q**
Enter Option: **P**
POST MESSAGE
Message title: **Okay Kerry**
Enter message now. No more than 30 lines,
enter "/EXIT" on a new line when done.

**We can read you loud and clear, the
question, I think, is can you read us?**

/EXIT

*He follows the directions and chooses the send option. The
system tells him the message has been posted, and he decides
to log off for now. . . .*

Send, Read, Edit, Abort: **Send**
  Message #32 posted.
    Enter Option: **O**
    Are you sure?   **YES**

= – Thank you for calling the PCD BBS – =
  Call again soon!

You can see that public bulletin-board systems, like this one, are
available to everyone, for whatever purpose they like. The operators
of these systems usually encourage any type of discussion, with the
exception of exchanging possibly illegal information.

A Hackers' BBS The next sample will give you a glimpse of what you are likely to see
on a typical hackers' bulletin-board system. The operators of these
systems try for a bit more security than the operators of average bulletin boards, but since the members are not expected to give their real
names or phone numbers, the security really isn't very good. In fact, it
quickly becomes hard to tell whether someone is using the board under one name or thirty. It is also usually very difficult, if not impossible, to tell what a person is like or who he – or she – is from a handle
alone. To show you what I mean, here is a typical example of the user
log of a hackers' BBS:

THE ANIMAL	HACKERS ANONYMOUS	DR. ATOMIC
EL BANDITO	MR. BIG	FLORIDA CRACKER
CAPTAIN CROOK	JOHN D. HINCKLEY	PROFESSOR FALKEN
SHORT FUSE	THE GHOST	MAJOR HAVOC
SIR HOAGY	BLACK KNIGHT	KARI LARSEN
TOM LAWLESS	THE LODE RUNNER	AUTO MAN

SAND MAN	MASSIVE MAX	THE MONITOR
THE OUTRIDER	THE SCORPIO	THE SKEPTOR
MIKE SMITH	STAN SMITH	STEVE SMITH
TOM SMITH	THE SPAZ	THE TYPIST
THE VICTOR	THE WASP	THE ZAP

Now, here are some typical messages from a hackers' BBS. Of course, names and numbers have been omitted, so they don't apply to anyone real. Many of the messages may strike you as confusing or technical and not too exciting, so my comments will try to explain what these hackers are talking about.

Just as hackers are known by their handles, so are bulletin boards. The County Jail is the name of this board — it's typical of a hacker BBS. Some computers, by the way, do not display lowercase characters. All text on this computer is uppercase only. . . .

YOU HAVE JUST ENTERED THE COUNTY JAIL
(SHOW YOUR BADGE OR TYPE: "NEW" > _ _ _ _ _ _
      ON-LINE: THE CRACKER
::::: WELCOME TO THE COUNTY JAIL :::::

     DISCLAIMER:
THE SYSOP OF THIS BOARD CAN'T BE HELD
RESPONSIBLE FOR ANYTHING POSTED BY ITS
USERS. SORRY GUYS.
YOUR LAWFULL FRIEND,

```
            = _ = _ = _ = _ = _ = _
\ _ _ _ _ \ T H E    S Y S O P  \ _ _ _ _ _ \
/         / = _ = _ = _ = _ = _ /         /
```

NO MAIL WAITING, SORRY.

= =

There is a secret level on this BBS. A user has to type ALBANY and a secret password to get to it. Other sections of this board would look a lot like the public BBS shown earlier. . . .

(? = MENU) COMMAND: **ALBANY**
PASSWORD?: **XXXXXX**

The hacker decides to read messages, beginning with #1. This message is about a computer, GIZMO, that can be accessed by the phone number and codes given by the hacker.

The # character used here replaces the digits of codes that would actually be posted on this BBS....

—> THE UNDERGROUND BOARD ACTIVE <—
TITLES, READ, QUIT: **READ 1**
MESSAGE #1:   GIZMO!
(SPACEBAR QUITS MESSAGE)
MSG. LEFT BY: HACKERS ANONYMOUS

I GUESS TRI-STATE MANAGES GIZMO SO TO
USE GIZMO, CALL 555-0000 USE CODE # # # # # #
OR # # # # # # LATER,

H.A.
PS DOES ANYONE KNOW IF GIZMO IS
A PART OF TRI-STATE?

HOW ABOUT GETTING SOME MESSAGES POSTED
ON THIS BOARD – PEOPLE – THANX!

The system tells the hacker there are 25 messages. The hacker requests message #2. This one tells him he can access a "stock quotes" system by calling 555-0000, entering the account name PALS, and the password 66C3P43V. Whoever left the message did not leave a "name"....

(1-25, LAST = 1, QUIT = Q) READ MSG.# **2**

MESSAGE #2: STOCK QUOTES
(SPACEBAR QUITS MESSAGE)
MSG. LEFT BY: ANONYMOUS
TO ACCESS STOCK QUOTES:
CALL 555-0000. AT THE PROMPT ENTER
"PALS" PW = '66C3P43V'
COME ON LETS GET POSTING!

FD

The hacker requests message #3. . . .

(1-25, LAST = 2, QUIT = Q) READ MSG.# **3**

*It's about a system named TREE-HOUSE. Someone named
THE PHREAK has found two more codes. . . .*

MESSAGE #3: MORE TREE-HOUSE
(SPACEBAR QUITS MESSAGE)
MSG. LEFT BY: ANONYMOUS

SOME MORE TREE-HOUSE CODES . . . ID RICK94
ID RAY84

MORE LATER . . . THE
>——PHREAK——<

(1-25, LAST = 3, QUIT = Q) READ MSG.# **4**

*This message, again from THE PHREAK, now asks for a little
help. . . .*

MESSAGE #4: LOCAL CRAN
(SPACEBAR QUITS MESSAGE)
MSG. LEFT BY: ANONYMOUS

DOES ANY BODY KNOW THE CRAN CODE LOCAL
TO NEW YORK? PLEASE HELP ME, THANX,
THE
>——PHREAK——<

(1-25, LAST = 4, QUIT = Q) READ MSG # **5**

A message giving some (altered) network addresses. . . .

MESSAGE #5: MORE CONNECTIONS
(SPACEBAR QUITS MESSAGE)
MSG. LEFT BY: ANONYMOUS

HERE ARE A FEW ADDRESSES FOR MEGANET:

. . . DILLA INC.   ### . . . NETPRI
. . . PRI-TEX   ### . . . PRI-TEX-A
. . . AUTOSL   ### . . . IBM 370

... E.L. MANAGER   ### ... C-C-A TEST

... D-CARE I   ### ... ?? (VAX)

... DITY SYSTEM   ### ... IRN DUST

... A.P.L. SYS   ### ... PSW>SYSTEM

... ?? IBM/370   ###(ALNA SP.)

(1-25, LAST = 5, QUIT = Q) READ MSG.# **6**

Here, some phone numbers and a little information about what system is on the receiving end. White Nite is another hackers' BBS. . . .

MESSAGE #6: MISC PH

(SPACEBAR QUITS MESSAGE)

MSG. LEFT BY: ANONYMOUS

HERE IS SOME JUNK I JUST RAN ACROSS:

000-555-0000 3 CODES NEEDED TO GET IN

000-555-0000 TESTLINK

000-555-0000 LON DIST 12 A

000-555-0000 O-TEST E-D

000-555-0000 MET COMPUTER

000-555-0000 CTCF SYSTEM

000-555-0000 S.H.L COMPUTER

000-555-0000 H.A.T. SYSTEM TWO

000-555-0000 NE-IND 12

000-555-0000 WHITE NITE

GET POSTING!

(1-25, LAST = 6, QUIT = Q) READ MSG.# **7**

Back to GIZMO. Once again the # replaces the digits of real codes. The hacker cautions others to use the old codes first, however, to lengthen the lifespans of both the old and new codes. . . .

MESSAGE #7: THE PHREAKS!

(SPACEBAR QUITS MESSAGE)

MSG. LEFT BY: ANONYMOUS

WHERE ARE ALL THE PHREAKS!? P.S. I HACKED

SOME MORE GIZMO CODES LAST NIGHT AND
HERE THEY ARE:
######
######
DON'T USE THEM UNTIL THE OLD ONES DIE!
THAT WAY WE WILL HAVE CODES THAT WORK
FOR A LONG TIME. COMPRENDE'?
HERE ARE THE OLD ONES THAT STILL WORK:
#######
USE THEM IN ORDER! OK???

(1-25, LAST = 7, QUIT = Q) READ MSG.# **8**

*Just after message #7, someone had asked whether ######
was still a valid code for GIZMO....*

MESSAGE #8: WHAT ABOUT?
(SPACEBAR QUITS MESSAGE)
MSG. LEFT BY: ANONYMOUS

WHAT ABOUT ###### FOR AN OLD GIZMO
CODE???

(1-25, LAST = 8, QUIT = Q) READ MSG.# **9**

*An invitation . . . "conferencing" is a kind of free-form electronic
meeting of hackers and phreaks who all get on the same circuit, so
they can all speak to one another – sometimes in groups of up to
twenty at a time. AE stands for ASCII Express, a BBS for trading
Apple software....*

MESSAGE #9: CONFERENCING
(SPACEBAR QUITS MESSAGE)
MSG. LEFT BY: DR. ATOMIC

IF ANYBODY WANTS TO GET IN ON SOME COOL
CONFERENCING, LEAVE ME YOUR VOICE # AND
WHO TO ASK FOR AND I'LL GIVE YA A CALL,
OR LEAVE A MESSAGE ON MY AE LINE
(555-0000) . . . WE USUALLY RUN 2 OR 3

CONFERENCES A DAY, BUT WE CAN MAKE
ROOM FOR MORE.... +DR. ATOMIC+

(1-25, LAST=9, QUIT=Q) READ MSG.# **10**

*Here are a few numbers that were found by a hacker using a modem
and a scan program. He offers speculation as to their purpose....*

MESSAGE #10: STRANGE COMPUTERS
(SPACEBAR QUITS MESSAGE)
MSG. LEFT BY: ANONYMOUS

HOW ABOUT SOME HELP WITH A FEW NUMBERS
MY SEARCH PROGRAM CAME UP WITH:
(IF YOU KNOW ANYTHING ABOUT THEM, JUST
LEAVE A MESSAGE)
555-0001 BELL TEST SIGNAL?
   " -0002 1200 BAUD?
   " -0003 (???) ˆE GETS A.B.
   " -0004 CARRIER BUT ??
   " -0005 1200 BAUD ONLY?
   " -0006 1200 BAUD ONLY?
   " -0007 (??) TRY HITTING TOUCH-TONES
   " -0008 STRANGE COMPUTER
   " -0009 1200 BAUD ONLY?
   " -0000 1200 #$%ˆ!ˆ!!#__

= CARRIER LOST =

*Oops, The hacker got disconnected. Bad telephone connections do
this at times....*

BULLETIN-BOARD SECURITY

Bulletin boards provide a valuable community service to all modem
users. They allow people to meet and exchange ideas or information,
or just to talk and socialize. Even though hackers who bother bulletin
boards are generally looked down upon by other hackers, sometimes
a bulletin board is still disrupted.

Most hackers would not find it too exciting to crack a bulletin
board – the computer involved is probably no bigger than their own,

180

the security is not all that great, and bulletin boards are run by dedicated computer hobbyists. People who haven't thought much about this, however, and who haven't actually tasted "real" hacking sometimes make this effort. But if a slight effort is made by the system operator, the odds are that any hacking activity could be averted – and this would be a great relief to many users of bulletin boards.

The problem with security on bulletin boards is that there are Crashers in the world, and most Crashers love to crash bulletin-board systems. When a Crasher crashes a bulletin-board system, he tries either to break out of the controlling BBS software or to get the system operator's password. In the latter case, as with many mainframes, password assignment is a security problem with BBS software. On some bulletin-board systems it is essentially no problem at all to guess the system operator's password, because of the well-known procedures used to assign it. Other techniques Crashers use on bulletin-board systems include entering an unexpected character in the right place (or the wrong place, depending on your point of view), entering a number that is too large for the system to handle, or overflowing the disk space by entering too many messages. Any of these tricks may, in a crashable BBS program, send the Crasher an error message and the system prompt . . . at which point he will have control over the computer system itself.

When the time comes, the Crasher will probably bring about his moment of glory by formatting the disks that are currently on the system, and since formatting a disk automatically erases all information on it, this means all messages that have not been backed up (in some cases, this is all of them) will be lost forever. Also, if the system operator does not have his bulletin-board software backed up, it too may be lost. If the Crasher is more inclined to be subtle (Crashers are not known for this), he may slowly start introducing problems into the BBS. In any event, and particularly if the BBS uses a hard disk, the importance of backups should be obvious.

The remaining few pages of this chapter are directed primarily at a fairly narrow group of people: the operators of bulletin-board systems. But even if you are not associated with bulletin boards at all, I think you will still find this information interesting. At the very least, you will learn more about the ways in which hackers and operators play off against one another. Here, then, are a few points to bear in mind on keeping bulletin-board systems secure.

Is it worth keeping secure? First of all, obvious as it sounds, think about whether the board is worth the effort. Some people run bulletin boards as a light hobby and don't want to spend very much time or work on security. That's fine, because a bulletin-board system really may not be worth the trouble of keeping secure, and certainly would not be worth an encryption scheme or a callback modem. On the other hand, if the information on the bulletin board has professional or other value, you would at least want to be certain that regular back-ups are made.

Don't follow a predictable pattern in assigning passwords. Password assignment procedures on bulletin-board systems are known to be quite poor. For example, a typical bulletin-board password might not even contain any random characters a hacker would have to guess at. Some of these passwords look just like the X7TLO password I used in the public bulletin-board example. At first glance, X7TLO might look as random as anything, but another password on the same system might be X43TLO. A quick examination of the bulletin-board program would tell any hacker that the passwords all consist of X, followed by a user number, followed by TLO. On such systems hackers also know that the operator is almost always user number 1.

Most systems using this password-assignment format now make one or more of the letters random. One random letter is no problem to hack; two or three are substantially more difficult in terms of time and the number of possible combinations.

Other systems have the users choose their own passwords – a good procedure, as long as they choose reasonably difficult ones to hack (as I've already mentioned many times). A few bulletin-board systems either don't use passwords or they make passwords optional. These systems are "open books" to hackers.

Filter the input. Most BBS software available today is fairly difficult to crash, but there is at least one in which it is possible for a hacker to use a control character in the title of a message. When the program tries to read the message, it crashes. This vulnerability can easily be fixed by "filtering" the characters that are input, so that only the displayable characters and the few necessary control characters, such as the end-of-line marker, are allowed to get through. This filtering might require some programming ability, since the operator may have to write a routine that would tell the computer, "Look at all input; allow this, this, and this character to get through, but trap any of the following characters...."

Make extensive use of error traps. The goal of a bulletin-board Crasher is to cause an error in the microcomputer, because he hopes that the computer will stop the current program, revert to the operating system, and give him the system prompt. In most languages, however, there is a way to trap these errors and keep the computer from turning control over to the Crasher. For example, in almost all versions of BASIC, there is a command called ON ERROR GOTO that works very well in most of these situations by telling the program to GOTO a special part of itself (an error-handling routine) that traps and takes care of errors rather than allowing those errors to cause problems and stop execution of the entire program.

Crash your own system. The only way you can really ensure that no Crasher will crash your system is to try crashing it yourself. I know of one sysop who set up his program and put messages up on all the other bulletin-board systems, tempting people to try attacking his system. After several weeks of this testing, he knew where all the weaknesses in his system were. By keeping track of all the tricks that the various Crashers had used to crash the system, he could fix these problems and use his program comfortably to run a public board without fear of it being crashed.

There is quite a bit of debate going on regarding bulletin-board sysops and the extent of their responsibility for their users. The whole issue is part of a rapidly changing area of the law, and system operators today have to be very wary of how their users use the bulletin-board services. Some bulletin-board system operators have had their systems taken away by the authorities because of illegal messages placed on the system by users. Others have been threatened with felony charges. BBS operators have been subjected to arrest and the first

Bulletin Boards
And the Law

stages of criminal prosecution, and in every case I know of so far, they have been given back their equipment before the case has gone to court. At this rate, as long as these cases are kept out of the courts and no judicial decision is handed down on the subject as a whole, raids on system operators can, and probably will, continue.

For myself, I feel that system operators who have their bulletin-board systems and equipment removed are being treated improperly. At times, they have their multithousand-dollar systems — which may be used for schoolwork or business, as well as a BBS — taken away for over a month. All because some unknown person placed a piece of information that is considered illegal on a bulletin board. I believe the system operator should not be held responsible for the acts of others, whom he doesn't even know. On the other hand, I must also admit that, as the proprietor of the system, the operator does have at least the right, and perhaps the obligation, to scan the board for illegal or offensive public postings he can then take steps to eliminate.

CHAPTER TEN

Telltale Signs

What with logic bombs, Trojan horses, decoy programs, telephone tricks, and all the other little techniques hackers know and use, you may, by now, think that there is no possible way to track down a good hacker. I've deliberately taken care to tell you about a lot of things that might be wrong with your computer security – things that might also seem difficult, if not impossible, to detect.

Owner, operator, or user of a large system, you may feel you are up against a new game: hacker-in-a-haystack. After all, even small or medium-sized systems contain a considerable number of files and are accessed a relatively large number of times every day by a variety of users. If you are working with a very large system, the problem can be magnified enormously. How can a system operator be expected to examine every file, every user, and every remote access? If this is close to what you are thinking, I've succeeded in expanding your awareness of computer security. Now it's time to see how you can take the initiative. Here's *your* advantage: Hackers leave footprints.

**TURNABOUT IS
FAIR PLAY**

Unless a hacker expends quite a bit of effort while demonstrating a high level of skill, he can't help but leave signs of his presence. Even in those cases where he could be a hundred percent undetectable, no hacker is going to bother becoming invisible. The sysop of the system under attack is the person who concerns the hacker the most, and in the real world ... some sysops don't care about security, others are very busy, still others think hackers are a bunch of kids who overestimate their own importance, and others (especially in the academic world) sympathize with, at least, the Student hacker's addiction to computers. So, whether the hacker's footprints consist of unexplained miscellaneous files, altered information, or strange communications, hackers rely on the fact that these signs will go unnoticed. They are correct about eighty-five percent of the time.

This fact can work in your favor if you use your computer's log files often and educate your users so they can help you look for the danger signs. The average hacker is going to be, at the very least, slightly careless on your system, because he isn't used to people actually caring about security. Use his trusting nature to your advantage.

**HOW THE USER
CAN HELP**

Hackers often give uneducated users all kinds of unusual signs and signals that they never even notice. At times, the way these signs are scattered all over the place, it seems that the users must be tripping over them constantly. If users knew what to look for, how to look for it, and what to do once they found it, there would be a much better chance of keeping hackers off the system. To help users, here are some "footprints" a user should look for.

Excessive log-on times. In many companies, employees do not have to charge their computer time to a specific project or even account for it. Sometimes, they are not even told how much time is spent on their accounts, and some never seem to use their authorized accounts. Because of this, if and when the employee logs on, he or she may not notice unauthorized activity on the account, even if the system displays the last log-on date, or the length of the last session.

Hackers know they can use such accounts for days at a time without the user noticing or keeping track of how often the account is used. For example, I remember one account that was heavily used by hackers. If the system, which had built-in accounting software, had charged the computer time used to one or more tasks or projects authorized on the user's account, it would have cost under $50 a month in most cases. Of course, this wasn't most cases. Hackers started using the system and adding up computer time which, as far as they were concerned, was free. Before too long, the monthly charge would have been over $5000 if anyone or anything had kept track. But because the user did not have to account for this time or charge it to an authorized job, he never had any idea. On the other hand, how could he?

Files that have been moved, deleted, or otherwise altered. No matter what his objectives, many of the things a hacker needs to do require modifying existing files. In almost every case, users don't notice the alteration of a file or two. These little alterations, however, can aid a hacker. They may, for instance, at some later date, result in triggering a Trojan horse that may change the user's password to something the hacker knows, and thus allow the hacker to log onto the user's account even after the user changes his password. Altered files could also be used to store information, so that the hacker would not have to create new, possibly detectable, files. At any rate, if there is a file on a user's account that has not been used in eight months, a hacker will feel fairly safe in altering it to use himself. Again, as I've said so often, user education is the key to avoiding this problem.

In addition, hackers can sometimes copy all of the important system files into the directory they are using so it is easier to learn about the files. Hackers may also copy files that interest them in other ways, again so they can look at all the interesting files without having to move around the system all the time.

The most likely type of file that a hacker will want to copy, however, will be "source files," if they are available to him. A source file is a text file that contains a computer program. The program, at this point, can be read and modified by a programmer, but to become "readable" to a computer, it must be "compiled" by a special program known, appropriately enough, as a compiler. Once a source file is compiled, it becomes a program that can then be run on that particular computer. A programmer writes programs by writing a source-code file and having this source code compiled. The source code is kept, and if any changes need to be made, they are made on the source code, which is then recompiled into a newer version of the program.

The hacker can take a source file and do one of two things: First, he can alter the file as a Trojan horse and recompile it. Second, he may simply be able to compile the program and run it himself. This may not sound valuable in itself, but it's possible that the hacker does not have the power to run the actual program. If he takes the source file and recompiles it, however, that sometimes opens the door for him.

Files that have been added. Hackers often need to create files. These files might consist of programs that store information (or passwords) or access various sections of memory, such as password buffers. Or, they might contain any of the programs that hackers use to obtain access to accounts. Unfortunately, most users are still somewhat computer timid, and will assume that they should not touch any files, even in their own accounts, that they didn't create. It's also likely that users will shrug off the existence of those files – even if they have such obvious names as PASSWD.HAK or HACKER.

On the other hand, funny things can happen when a user does get curious, too. Earlier in the book, I told you of a hacker who used a file named TOP SECRET as bait – everyone who tried this file was treated to a silly message and, unwittingly, helped the hacker find his or her password. In a similar instance, there was no bait, but I know a user who did wonder about some strange files listed under his directory. Among them, he found one called PASS1, so he decided to try it. He typed PASS1, and then assumed something must not be happening correctly, because all the file did was display WORKING...on the screen. He didn't realize that, in typing the file name, he had started a program that was busy trying to get the system operator's password.

Directories that have been added. To hide a number of added files he wants to keep, a hacker may create a subdirectory within a user's directory. The hacker's subdirectory would be unobtrusively named, perhaps with only a single character, or "hidden" if the system allows such things to be done. Then, too, some systems allow non-printable characters as file names. These, of course, while they would be part of a directory, would not be displayed or printed as visible characters.

Older versions of a file. Some systems allow a user to keep several different versions of a file under the same file name. When a user tries to run, type, or edit the file, the system automatically chooses the newest version, unless the user specifies another. A hacker can use this feature to his advantage by giving his subdirectory or file the same name as an existing file belonging to the legitimate user. But the hacker would give his file an *earlier* version number. The result would be that anyone wanting to use the hacker's version would have to request it specifically. For example, there can be two different files, both called NOTES. One of them, NOTES;2, may be the user's daily notes to himself. The other, NOTES;1, could be the hacker's file. If the hacker wants to use his version of NOTES, he simply tells the system to use the version NOTES;1.

Strange electronic mail. Hackers may use two or more accounts to communicate among themselves. If the hackers know what they are doing, they stick to accounts that are unused. If the hackers don't know what they're doing, they sometimes communicate through accounts that are being used regularly by their rightful owners. In this case, a message meant to be read by a hacker may be sent to a user, instead. Almost always, though, a user will simply answer the strange mail with I DON'T UNDERSTAND or YOU'VE GOT THE WRONG PERSON. This warns the hacker that the account is in use.

Most systems also have a special program that allows two or more people to carry on a conversation through their terminals. Hackers like to use these programs too (and may create their own, if none exists) to communicate with each other. Sometimes a hacker inadvertently contacts an authorized user, who may be surprised by a message like JOE? IS THAT YOU? The user often assumes the message is a mistake and ignores it, although such an incident is even harder to explain if the message is MR. MIDNIGHT? IS THAT YOU?

Lost or pre-read electronic mail. Sometimes hackers read a user's electronic mail, so this is another "footprint" users can learn to watch for. Most electronic-mail systems have a feature that gives the user a list of all the mail that has not been read. If a hacker reads the mail first, the user may never see his new mail, because the system will keep saying that there is none. And even if the user goes back, checks old mail, and finds messages that look unfamiliar, the user will usually just assume that the computer messed up or that he or she has forgotten what was there. It is quite possible on most such systems to read someone else's mail and keep the system from changing the status from "new mail" to "old mail," but most hackers wouldn't bother, simply because most hackers don't say anything, anyway.

The Oversimplified System

As something of a side issue, sometimes a user who links up with a network computer doesn't notice signs of hacking for a very simple reason, despite the fact that the hacker who uses the person's account thinks the user must be blind: The user's machine does too much automatically. A user may have a personal computer set up as a smart terminal and, literally at the push of a button, he or she can simply tell the terminal, "Bring my new mail back to me and send this mail out to these people." The terminal will then call the system, enter the user's name and password, issue the commands needed to retrieve all of the user's incoming mail, and issue the commands needed to send all of the outgoing mail to other users.

Such a system is usually set up by a consulting company that advertises an electronic-mail system so simple that anyone can use it with no expensive training. To back up its claim, such a company does not teach the user anything more difficult than how to turn on a terminal and hit a few appropriate keys.

Granted, such a "smart" terminal is a boon to the busy user, but in these cases, there is not much chance of the user spotting hacker activity, because he or she never sees anything of the procedures involved in logging on and off or sending and receiving mail. Because the password is stored in the personal computer, the user may not even know it exists, much less have any idea about how to change it. The user may not even realize that the actual mail computer is hundreds or thousands of miles away. If asked, the user might guess that, somehow, the microcomputer handled it all.

This type of an overautomated system has one additional requirement beyond user awareness of the hacker "footprints" I've mentioned. To the point of redundancy, *educate the user.* Assume that this person is interested in the technology being used – perhaps not at the level of bits, bytes, or BASIC, but almost certainly at the level of how the call is originated, how the main computer recognizes the user, or how one person's mail is kept separate from everyone else's, and so on. The more comfortable people are with the equipment they use, the more likely they are to notice idiosyncrasies that occur, and the more likely they are to use the equipment correctly.

Users should be told whom to see if they notice any signs of hacking on their accounts. The system operators need this feedback, for one thing because they may already be in contact with the hackers. If they know more about the hackers' activities, or are told that they are destroying data, the system operators may be in a good position to monitor the hackers, remove their accounts, have them traced, ask them to leave, or take further steps to make the system less accessible.

Taking the Initiative

    It may be dangerous to tell a user to change his or her password and forget the matter, because in some cases, it is simple for a hacker to alter the command that changes a password. Instead of just changing the password, the command will record the request to change the password, record the new password, and store the information in a file for the hacker. The hacker may then log on later, read the file that has recorded both the request and the new password, and change the password for the user. This trick works well for the hacker. Not only does he learn the new password, but if the user tries to log on again, before the hacker has a chance to change the password, the user always tries his old one. I am not telling users not to change passwords, but I am saying that they should also notify someone about it.

No matter how well educated they are about security, some users will continue to miss the signs that hackers are using their accounts. Some may also feel that it is not their job to spot hacker activity – that the role belongs to the system operators, and that users aren't properly trained. To some degree, they're right, but it is a dangerous attitude from the computer owner's point of view. After all, in an analogous situation, the police do what they can to keep intruders out of a house, but the final responsibility rests with the people who live there.

THE SYSTEM OPERATOR'S ROLE

Fortunately, with most systems, the security-conscious system operator/programmer/security manager should have little trouble in spotting a hacker's footprints. Here are some things to look out for. They fall into two categories: everything discussed to this point...and then some.

Hacker signs already mentioned. An operator is a user before he's an operator. Whether he simply watches his own account or takes it upon himself to watch or spot-check other accounts, he should watch for the signs I have listed for users as if he were a user himself. System operators can be almost as blind as users in some cases, and they don't have any excuse.

There are, by the way, some system operators who *allow* hackers limited use of a computer system as a way of keeping them under control. These operators are not the same as those who do not see the signs of hackers. I've known of some very, very good system operators who have allowed hackers limited use of their systems. As far as I can tell, none of these systems suffered any damage as a result.

An overused account. If hackers have access to only one or two accounts on a computer, there are likely to be two or three hackers on the same account at any given time. Five or ten at a time is not rare, and even twenty would not surprise me. As I mentioned in an earlier chapter, a hacker can often break one account into several sub-accounts. In addition, hackers could run a bulletin board off your mainframe, allowing ten, twenty, even thirty people at a time to use the board – and all of them would be logged onto the same account. A system operator is in a very good position to see and act on this type of activity, but it's surprising how often hackers manage to get away with such group-access times.

A few systems help control this type of situation simply by limiting the number of people who are allowed to log onto an account at one time. And one system I know of automatically shuts down an account if more than five people are logged on at one time. When I last checked in, this system had not yet closed down on an authorized user, but it had closed down on several hackers. If nothing else, this type of system would make hackers become very careful of the number of people using one account.

Unusual times of activity. Hackers are well known and well publicized for their strange hours of activity. Any unusual activity times should be questioned. Bear in mind, though, that hackers don't always hack in the middle of the night. Depending on normal patterns of use, in some cases, activity during a lunch hour should be regarded as odd.

In one blatant example I know of, a system normally had an average of three users between 8 p.m. and 8 a.m. and an average of thirty-five users between 9 a.m. and 6 p.m. The system operators didn't seem to notice anything – or at least they didn't do anything – even when hackers started raising the average 8 p.m. to 8 a.m. figure to just under twenty users. It should have been quite clear what was going on.

Users of certain accounts going to strange places. If someone using a word-processing account is wandering around the accounting files, the password file, and the operator's files too much, question the person assigned to the account. Hackers like to move around, seeing as much of the system as they can, while users generally have plenty to do just dealing with their own work. Thus, hackers will look through as many files as they can while they are logged onto one account; word processors will deal with their own files.

Excessive use of the HELP files. The first time a hacker uses a particular system, he may resort to the HELP files for advice quite often. Most hackers do not want to spend thousands of dollars for all the various mainframe user's manuals, so they may even print out all of the HELP files the first time they have access to them.

An operator should be able to tell if the user of a particular account has spent three hours in the HELP files. Some system operators have been known to turn the tables on hackers and put a few tantalizing false entries into the HELP files – entries like SECRET or HACK. When a person asks for help on the topic, the system notifies the system operator. Because hackers use the HELP files more than users do, they are much more likely to come across these false entries.

Attempts to hack a password. This is the obvious sign: Note excessive numbers of unsuccessful log-on attempts. In many cases, an operator will ignore these attempts, because he doesn't quite know what to do about them. In most cases, this is fine. The system hasn't been penetrated, so what can you do but ignore such hacking?

A system operator should watch these attempts, though, in case the hacker does get through. He should also pay attention to the accounts and passwords the hacker is working on, to check for the possibility that inside help might have been involved.

THE NEXT STEP

Once users and system operators know what to look for and are diligently watching for signs of hacker infiltration, what are they to do with any information they find? For the user, the answer is usually simple enough: Back up any data to protect against loss, and tell the system operator as soon as possible. In most cases, the system operator, as the person who set up all the accounts and watches over them, is fairly well known to the users. If it seems likely – as in a very large company, for example – that users may not know the name and phone number of the person to call, make certain that person, and any special procedures for contacting him or her, are readily available.

System operators have a little more trouble and a few more options to choose from in handling hackers. They must use all the information they can gather. There is no one right way to proceed in all cases, but the next chapter will offer some advice on what to do with the hacker you've caught. You might say these methods have been field-tested for effectiveness.

CHAPTER ELEVEN

What to Do with the Hacker You've Caught

Finding evidence of hacker penetration is one thing, like finding out that your house has been burglarized while you were gone. But sooner or later you are going to encounter a "hot prowl" – an online, realtime, live-action intrusion by a hacker. And when you first encounter a hacker, it is vital to know how to handle him. A warlike attitude on your part, plus a misworded warning, plus a hacker who can and will harm your system could equal disaster. In addition to knowing the best approach to take with a hacker, you must also know how to identify, confront (if necessary), enlist (if possible), neutralize, and safely remove him.

Once a hacker is on your system, do you know what steps to take to eliminate him? In most cases I've come across, the honest answer is "No." Operators usually just kick a hacker off the system by hanging up the phone line and then killing the account he is using. While this

**HANDLING
A HACKER**

simple step sometimes works, and may be the best solution – with a Novice, for example – very often you will find that the hacker is kicked off only to come back to life under a different account name. Or you may afterward find out, to your dismay, that while he was on, your hacker set up a logic bomb to erase data at a later date or on his order.

Hackers are like electronic ghosts, in a way – they don't leave just because you want them to, and they can come back to "haunt" you. So, it is generally not a good idea to blindly throw a hacker off a system without asking a few questions first. A direct encounter with a hacker, if handled properly, can yield invaluable information about the security system's vulnerabilities.

A Case of Mishandling

There was once a system on which I had managed to get one account. One of the system operators discovered me after about two months and said that hackers were not allowed on "his" system. He suggested that I hang up and not call back. I said I would try, and added that he should be sure to kill the account I had been using.

After waiting a few days (a very long time for a hacker to wait), I called back. When I tried to use the account I had been using before, the computer sent me a message along the lines of, "You were told not to log onto this system again. Now leave and don't ever come back."

Well, I took it rather personally and decided to get back onto the system – a job that was almost too easy, because the operator had insisted on keeping the account active, so that he could leave me this clever message. It was no problem to bypass the program left behind to give me this message. Rather than hunt for another route, I got onto the system through the operator's own loophole.

After I did this, the operator wanted very much to talk to me, and even tried a female user to get me to call in. But I decided that I didn't want to talk to him. He did not take my advice to kill the account in the first place, he did a poor job by leaving me that message, and on top of that, he had been insulting. Many hackers cause trouble for less reason.

If he does decide to come back for a second try, a mishandled hacker may be interested in making his mark (read "cause trouble") on your system before you catch him a second time. But even if he is not interested in revenge, he will be a little more careful about wasting a valuable account, so he will try a little harder to avoid detection the second time around.

As the preceding story shows, attitude has a great deal to do with whether you handle a hacker poorly or well. It will be easy for me to tell you how not to foul things up. It will take more effort on your part to understand your opponent well enough to defeat him.

Thinking Like A Hacker

In Chapter Five, I mentioned a hacking strategy that I called "thinking like a user." The same strategy, in reverse, can help any system operator. Before you make any attempt to communicate with a suspected hacker, put yourself in his place and think like a hacker.

Like anyone else, hackers do not take kindly to people who take them for fools. Conversely, they won't hesitate to take you for a fool if everything you do or say convinces them that this is true. Regardless of what you think of hackers, remember that they are probably self-taught, definitely addicted to computers, and, at least sometimes, justifiably proud of what they know.

If you treat a high-level hacker contemptuously, your under-estimation of his ability could cost you dearly. At the same time, if you overestimate a Novice, you don't stand to lose much and will certainly make him feel good. Never underestimate the consequences of under-estimation: It is far safer to assume intelligence in your counterpart and to heave a sigh of relief when you discover a beginner than it is to treat as a Novice a hacker who actually has your system mined.

A hacker, especially a Student, has little reason to "play fair," much less reason to offer you his assistance, if he doesn't respect you. And the only way you can win his respect is by demonstrating your own intelligence. All but the wildest rogue Crashers respect intelligence, and a little thought will spare you vengeful and mischievous damage to your system. If you play your role effectively, you could lead the hacker to suspect that you are willing to play a game – which brings us to a second rule for thinking like a hacker: Treat your hacker as if he were your opponent in a devious game.

If you think "play it like a game" isn't a "mature" approach to a serious problem, I would suggest, from four years of experience, that you are already playing a game the moment you make contact with a hacker. Recognizing that the hacker treats hacking – and his contacts with you – as a game is the only way you can win. If exploration is the activity that proves curiosity is a major part of a hacker's personality, then game playing is the activity that gives you important information about the way a hacker views the world.

Many hackers, including me, are dedicated game players: chess, adventure games like Dungeons and Dragons, video games, hacking games – in varying degrees, they are all examples of attractive and intense pastimes that keep high-school hackers up all night.

Remember, chess is a game, but it can be a very serious one. So is hacking – to a hacker. To borrow a chess term to underscore my point, let's say: Choose your gambit thoughtfully, and make sure it's a good one, suited to you, your situation, and your opponent. Your immediate objective is to keep your system's data and its security intact. Your ultimate goal is to make your system security stronger. You want to win. With hacking, that means you need to talk to a hacker in such a way that you will gain his respect. You have to find a way to turn your opponent into a colleague.

LINES OF COM-
MUNICATION

Operators who want to talk to a hacker will usually try to get his phone number, thinking either that it would be nice to be able to call him anytime for security help, or that it would be nice to "have something" on him. If the hacker knows what he's doing, he won't give you his name or phone number, and any attempt to trace his call will fail. If you are dealing with a bright ten-year-old, which is a distinct possibility, crude threats might work, and silly ploys might yield a legitimate telephone number. But if your hacker is seventeen and thinks, rightly or not, that he's smarter than you are, a crude approach will net you nothing and may cause you grief sooner or later.

The solution is to chat with the hacker through the computer, allow the hacker to call you, or let the hacker give you a "test loop" to call. (A test loop is a set of two numbers the phone company uses. If each of you calls one of the numbers in the set, you will be able to speak to one another, without having to give out your real numbers).

He may even decide to give you a test loop as his phone number without telling you what it is.

In order to preserve data and maintain or enhance system security, you must first be aware of the danger posed by the hacker. Is sensitive information or a large amount of money at stake? How much is time on your computer worth to you and others? How "public" is your system? This is the background that the questions in Chapter Six were designed to provide. Without a knowledge of what you have to lose, you'll be handicapped from the start.

If you intend to use this encounter to strengthen your system, you have to follow a five-phase plan. Contacting a hacker, and thus tipping him off that you're "onto him" before you have a plan and a few alternate strategies in mind strongly diminishes your chances of success. I already mentioned the steps you need to take, in the order they should be taken: Identify, confront, enlist, neutralize, and remove the hacker from your system.

≡ *You need to* **identify** *a hacker if you hope to avoid the lengthy and laborious process of sifting through all of your user accounts to learn which ones are phony.*

≡ *In order to find out what you need to know, you usually have to* **confront** *the hacker. This is where the delicate and potentially rewarding game begins. Now, it's your ability as a game player, your ability to put yourself in the hacker's shoes, that's needed.*

≡ *If you confront the hacker correctly, you can then attempt to* **enlist** *his efforts in bolstering your defenses.*

≡ *When you know enough, you can* **neutralize** *the hacker and his works. This means more than locking him out; it also requires a determination of what other damage might have been done, or might be planned for the future.*

≡ *Then, you can* **remove** *him when you've found out what you need to know and your dialogue is over.*

199

TALKING TO YOUR HACKER

A good example of how not to open a conversation with a hacker was shown in the story of Al, the MegaCar system operator at the beginning of this book. Al started his dialogue with an aggressive statement: "We know who you are and what you did. Either cooperate or we will press full charges." With a different attitude and just a simple alteration of wording, Al might have steered the conversation down a much more rewarding path. He might have profited more by saying, "OK, you've told us you are in here. Now we sure would like to know how you managed to do it."

If it is convenient, you should try to talk to a hacker before you throw him off your system. If he is at all reasonable, you stand to gain quite a bit. But once you've decided to try to talk to him, how do you go about striking up a conversation? What do you say? How do you get him on your side?

It turns out that most system operators who decide to try to negotiate with a hacker do a good job of getting information out of him. You shouldn't shy away from learning what you need to learn. Hackers are out to learn, too. They like to exchange information – but not with anyone who is belligerent. Your approach will depend on your hacker and how well (or badly) you manage to communicate with one another, but here is a list of your objectives, along with possible techniques and possible responses from your "quarry."

Identify

Find out if this is a hacker or the actual account holder. Assume that the account holder's name is John; a simple question, like "Eric, is that you?" or "Do you have those reports done yet, Eric?" may do the trick. If it does, it will probably work out better than anything else, because the hacker will answer, and you will know he is a hacker, but he will *not* know that you are aware of who he is.

On the other hand, John may well have some files – letters, for example – in his account that gave his name away to the hacker. If you suspect this is true, a very good alternative is "What is your phone number?" or "What is your address?" These questions will alert a hacker right away, but any information known to both the user and operator, but not to a hacker, will help you confirm the identity of the person on the account. The hacker may, however, if he's really serious about your computer, find out in advance such things as the account holder's name, phone number, wife's name, and so on.

When you try to identify a hacker, one possible answer you may receive might be something along the lines of "I am not John. I'm a hacker." If this happens, there is a good chance, as you've seen elsewhere in this book, that the hacker is a Novice. Just as you should never discount the possibility of security penetration by a high-level hacker like one of the Inner Circle, you should never dismiss the (perhaps humiliating) possibility that a Novice could have cracked your security. It might help to keep in mind that the June 1983 report of the Canadian House of Commons' subcommittee on computer crime mentioned successful penetrations of the data banks of Canadian companies and the government by a group of eight-year-old hackers.

Determine the hacker's motives. In this area, a system operator shifts the questions toward the hacker himself, for the first time actually letting the hacker know that he has been discovered. Questions like "Why do you like our system?" or "What interests you most about our system?" are likely to get good results here. These are seductive questions to any self-respecting hacker, and he will usually be strongly tempted to "chat" about his personal hacking philosophy with the operator of a system he has cracked. After all, security is the bond between you and the hacker. No matter what his motives, you and he are both interested in the characteristics of your computer system that allowed him to break in.

Confront

Discover how the hacker got in. It would be nothing less than foolhardy to throw a hacker off without finding out how he got in. If you don't know how the hacker got into your system, ask. In fact, this is one of the few questions that almost any hacker will answer if you ask, although his response, unless he respects you, is likely to be a very general statement, such as, "You assign your passwords all wrong."

Your opponent has no reason to tell you anything truly helpful until you convince him that you are worthy of his information. To help in this regard, ask your question along the lines of, "Can you let me know what you did to get in?" If you ask in another way, you may give him the impression that you think he has no choice but to answer. In fact, he does have a choice – he has many: He can disappear and leave you scratching your head, he can refuse to talk to you, he can tell other hackers, he can damage data . . . you don't want to push him into any of them. Whether you like it or not, at this point, you are still playing a defensive game. You have to deal with your hacker as a respected opponent, not a hated enemy, if you hope to gain his cooperation. And his cooperation, by the way, *can* be valuable. I know one system operator who uncovered a major bug in a major operating system by asking a hacker how he got in, and because of this, the operator ended up with a much better job with the company that wrote the operating system. Bear this in mind: The hacker sees and exploits the "underside" of your system – the normal routes of access are closed to him.

A final note on this subject: At the other end of the capability spectrum, you may encounter a hacker who doesn't seem to know how he got in. If this true, there is a chance someone else did the work. Careful questioning may lead you to a much higher-level hacker.

Assess his attitude toward your system. It is nice to know whether the hacker respects your system or thinks it's "a piece of cake." Many system operators will already know the answer to this question because of the previous conversation or from clues left by the hacker's account activity. If his attitude is unknown, however, it is worth asking a question like, "So how does our system compare to the other systems you have used?" Be prepared for an honest answer.

Along the same lines, it is also definitely worth trying to find out if your hacker is just waiting for a chance to get back on your system and kill, kill, kill, or if he is just as happy to move on. You will find that most hackers are willing to move on down the road, but a few in every crowd will want to keep using *your* system. Fewer still will want to damage your system, but at least forewarned is forearmed.

Did he leave another way to get in? If you can, try to find out about any trapdoors or spare accounts the hacker may have left for himself. A hacker wouldn't be a hacker if he didn't try to create some alternate point of entry while he was on a system. A hacker can't help trying to log on again, even if he promises not to try. A good system operator may, *if* he asks right, even be able to talk a hacker into disclosing any alternate points of entry.

Invite the hacker to become a temporary consultant. If you are consider-   *Enlist*
ing this as a possibility, the hacker has already been a consultant to
some degree. If he has impressed you with his knowledge at this point,
you will probably want to talk to him in greater depth. A question
phrased something like, "You seem to know what you're talking about,
would you like to help us out a bit more?" should break the ice.

    If you haven't considered enlisting your hacker, consider this: As
far as access to your system is concerned, there is little room for debate. If the hacker got in, there is a security problem. Very likely, he
could help you see just where your security system needs work. Many
companies find consulting a hacker in this way very valuable. Some
have hired hackers for pay, but most find that a hacker who is willing to
help is generally willing to help for free. Hackers like talking to system
operators, and system operators often find the exchange worthwhile.
I (and many of my friends) have talked to rooms full of programmers
by speakerphone – a service for which a consultant might charge hundreds or even thousands of dollars.

    Would he be willing to help you keep the number of hackers down?
Some companies find it worthwhile to provide accounts on their system to one or more "trusted" hackers. These accounts are watched
carefully, and in exchange the hacker agrees to keep his friends away
from that particular computer. Even if you don't want to provide the
hacker with an account, you should still ask the hacker if he would be
willing to keep others off for free. Your chances are slim if you don't
offer anything in return, but the service can be valuable and is well
worth asking for, anyway.

Up to now I have touched on quite a few things I suggest you do. In   *A Few Don'ts*
many places I have implied or even said that you shouldn't do certain
things. Here is a list of things you don't want to do.

    Don't tell him he has no choice. As I said earlier, in most cases by
far the hacker does have a choice. If he never intended to help you
anyway, even if you asked in a nonaggressive manner, then saying this
won't help. If, as is usually the case, he did intend to talk to you, then
implying that the hacker's choices are very limited will do nothing but
hurt your cause. Many, many system operators have told hackers that

there was no way out. But hackers usually know when they should be worried and when they should not. They also know that system operators who *are* planning to press charges aren't going to talk about it.

Don't try to use a woman's name to get the hacker to call in. For starters, I'm sure it won't be long before more girls take up hacking, and then how are you to know who's at the other end of the line? Second, this is a very old trick and most hackers are only insulted by it.

Some system operators even get a woman to talk to a hacker while the operator is on another phone listening in. This is really silly, because the speaker is kept busy trying to figure out what to ask the hacker from the operator's hand signals. It doesn't sound very good.

Don't demand the hacker's phone number or address. This is another area in which the hacker has the advantage. He can just hang up at any time, so you shouldn't expect him to give his number to you. Some operators have been known to say, "We have you traced" and then, "Give us your phone number" in the same breath ... Bravo.

Don't bother mentioning the possible legal charges. Unless you plan on pressing charges (in which case, you'll want to keep it quiet), don't bother telling the hacker. He has heard the same thing many times before, and he knows that these threats always seem to be followed by "... but we'd rather take care of our security problems ourselves."

THE FINAL STAGES

Once you have succeeded in identifying, confronting, and possibly enlisting your hacker, you now have some very valuable information. But the value of that same information will be reduced to zero if you don't use what you know. Rather than kick your hacker off the minute you're satisfied that he's told you enough, it's better to let those accounts you know about exist for a short while longer in order to make sure that you get them all when you decide to act.

You must determine the extent of damage, if any, pinpoint booby traps or soft spots your opponent knows about, seal off sensitive areas of programs or data, and prepare yourself for every conceivable counterattack *before* you attempt to remove your hacker from your system. And when you do decide to cut him off, you must be sure to do it in a way that gives him the fewest options for effective countermeasures.

To this point, let's say you know there is a hacker on your system. You also have a good idea about how much trouble he is willing to go to in order to maintain access to your system. Hopefully, you know how he feels about your system, so you have either a sense of security or a sense of fear, depending on his attitude. If your talk was productive, then you also know the basic weak points that the hacker exploited. If you had a really good discussion, you may have some pointers from the hacker regarding the enhancement of your security. Now you can begin neutralizing him.

Draw up a list of accounts the hacker knows about. Proper use of the system logs can work well in this area. Other ideas that have worked include having all of your users log off every other hour so you can see who is left, killing accounts, one by one, known to be owned by the hacker (to see where he pops up next), and, of course, asking for them from the hacker himself.

Neutralize

    Go over your list of any and all pieces of advice that the hacker gave you. If he did give you any advice, follow it. Hackers often tell system operators all they need to know in order to secure a system well enough to keep hackers out and away. What you must remember is this apparent willingness to cut off their own access to your system stems from hackers' assurance, often reinforced by experience, that sysops often either fail to understand what they are being told or, for one reason or another, fail to take the hackers seriously. The hackers are pretty certain they can try again, and they usually succeed, because the sysops did not do everything the hacker advised them to do or because they did a poor job.

    Check for any possible trapdoors, logic bombs, or Trojan horses. In many cases, you will be able to tell, from your conversation and what you know of the hacker's activity, whether your hacker is good enough at manipulating your system to know how to do these things. If you feel that he is good enough, you will want to be very careful about finding any traps. The best way to find them is to look closely at the files under the directory or directories that the hacker used, because a hacker quite often doesn't get around to erasing the files he used to create the tools he needed.

Remove   When you are reasonably certain you have identified all the illegal accounts and have searched the system thoroughly for trapdoors and logic bombs, it is time to actually throw the hacker off the system.

You will now have to decide what type of hacker you have on your system. If he seems reasonable (a Student, perhaps), you will want to wait until the hacker returns and is online (connected with the system). Once he is, you should diplomatically let him know that you plan to throw him off. Most operators handle this quite well by telling the hacker that the owner of the system, the operator's boss, is getting upset at the unauthorized accesses and that they cannot continue. In this way you are again treating the hacker as an intelligent opponent and are trying to keep him cooperative, even as you declare that the game is over.

In other cases, however, when the hacker is more volatile or destructive, it is best not to talk to him, because of the danger of further motivating him toward a destructive act. With this type of hacker, you can only hope that the procedures you go through in removing him and denying him further access are done very well.

Whether or not you talk to the hacker, the process of throwing him off is usually fairly simple. Almost always it is just a matter of eliminating the accounts involved or changing their passwords.

Now, it's time for a quarantine. Watch the system closely for at least a week afterward, to map any further hacker activity. It would be a great help during this period if users could be told not to use the system, but this request is almost always unreasonable. Even if your system remains in use, however, if you watch it for a week or more, you are very likely to see the hacker try to get back on. If you don't already know, you will get a good idea of how he got onto your system in the first place. You will also stand a very good chance of heading him off if he succeeds again. If he doesn't appear to make another attempt, you are probably okay...then again, there is sometimes good reason to be paranoid when a hacker *appears* to stop trying. If he was very, very good.... Ah, well, security *is* an ongoing concern.

Epilogue

I don't know if "right makes might," but in my case, at least, that's very true. On the afternoon of October 13, 1983, several gentlemen representing the Federal Bureau of Investigation ended my career as a hacker and put The Cracker into permanent retirement. For those of you who may be curious, I'll outline the details here. But first . . . just a little bit of background.

Computer security today is the focus of one rapidly changing area of the law. To hackers, what is known as "browsing" is a (usually) harmless, "educational" pursuit. In the past year or so, however, I've come to realize that browsing raises some legal and ethical questions, such as: What constitutes invasion of privacy? What are the rights and privileges of the individuals involved? On a more technical level, to what degree are computer memory and electronically coded data entitled to protection under the law?

Such questions are now being considered at both the state and federal levels, and laws are changing to meet the challenge posed by hackers. New attitudes toward browsing are emerging, and I'm certain that hacking, as I practiced it, will soon be universally considered a crime – perhaps not as severely punished as more "traditional" computer crimes, but just as wrong.

Back in the "old days" of 1983, however, while hacking wasn't right, it wasn't exactly wrong, either. And when I was arrested, it was on charges of wire fraud, because no other federal law was applicable.

HOW I GOT CAUGHT

I was living at home, with my parents and family, when the doorbell rang on that Thursday afternoon. But I wasn't completely surprised to see two gentlemen standing in the doorway with their identification and their warrants. The night before, I had called another member of the Inner Circle, and he had told me his computer equipment, floppy disks, and even his telephones had been seized a few hours earlier. Altogether, I later found out that Federal agents had visited at least nine members of the Inner Circle, in eight different states, on the preceding day, October 12th.

After I looked at their identification and read their warrants, the two gentlemen on the front porch were joined by several colleagues. They entered my house and searched the premises, and, in the process, confiscated all computer equipment, any electronic equipment they did not understand, magnetic disks and tapes, my telephone, and all my notes and written logs. Two or three took notes and made an inventory of the computer equipment they were taking.

During this visit, I was asked a number of questions – did I ever transfer funds, who were my friends, did I ever damage anything, did I have any black friends, had I sold any secret information – and I was told that I was one of several people around the country involved in an FBI investigation regarding unauthorized use of the computer that was in charge of a service called Telemail, which is accessible from the GTE Telenet network service.

Telenet and Telemail

Telenet is one of the large public networks. When companies link their computer systems to Telenet, a user only needs to call the network to access the computer. The charge is often lower than a long-distance phone call would be, and is normally charged to the computer being called – not to the caller. Telemail is an electronic-mail system that is also owned by GTE. Many large corporations use Telemail's services as an electronic-mail system, so that their employees around the country can easily communicate with one another.

One day, a GTE customer told a hacker about a default password for user accounts that, as usual, was not changed very often by the users. User accounts only send mail back and forth, so this information was not too useful. Still, I obtained a Telemail account in mid-1982, and other hackers were also aware of this vulnerability for over a year.

There is (or was) a more interesting aspect to Telemail, however. When a corporation uses Telemail as its electronic-mail system, it is given a special account known as an administrative, or "admin" account, that gives the user the power to create other accounts. The person who has the admin account is, in effect, a system operator, and uses the account to create accounts for all the people who will be using the mail system. There are hundreds of these admin accounts, each one controlling as many as several hundred users.

Eventually, some hacker decided that it would be worthwhile to get an admin account. Using a typical user's account, he was able to get a list of all the admin accounts...very obligingly furnished by the system at the hacker's request, complete with first and last names of the owners. Members of the Inner Circle and other hackers then tried out hundreds of different admin accounts, using the owner's first name as a password. In a few cases, this simple scheme worked.

I became the "owner" of an admin account in November 1982, and through the end of the year, I kept busy learning how to use it. During this time, I could have read private bulletins placed by NASA, Raytheon, Bell Labs, the Jet Propulsion Laboratory, and most of the other Telemail subscribers. (I didn't, of course – NASA and the others are pretty big, and I prefer to think I'm not foolish.)

Between about January and June 1983, I did nothing more with my admin account. During this time, there were only a few (about ten to fifteen) hackers using Telemail. Then, in August, other hackers and I used our admin accounts to create our own bulletin-board system. Word spread, and eventually more than forty hackers used Telemail to communicate with one another. A few, who had admin accounts, set up accounts for other users.

Then, we began to realize there was something strange about this system: It was not set up in the way most hackers were accustomed to. When a hacker went to look for a system operator, he found that there was no system operator to talk to. No one with more power than the admins seemed to exist.

It was as if Telemail were a ghost town. There seemed to be no humans running the place – just the computer system, watching over the admins who, in turn, watched over the users. Although the users of admin accounts had more power than anyone else, there *had* to be a still more powerful sysop's account, with control over all the admins. But no matter how hard we tried, we could find no system operator.

After several months, we began to feel no one cared about us. We had heard that Telemail served about twenty-five thousand people. Was it possible that forty hackers were not noticed at all? We were only 0.16 percent of the total, so it seemed quite possible.

But acceptance of that hypothesis led to our downfall.

Caught
If you are not extremely careful and self-observant, very soon you stop thinking like a hacker. Hackers who were using Telemail started to get a little careless. At least one left his name or phone number on the system. Another made the mistake of writing GTE a letter that offered to help solve Telemail's security problem. Three months later, thanks to word of mouth, there were one- to two-hundred hackers on the Telemail system.

As a result, the FBI was called in and eventually started raiding the houses of the people they could track down. I was told some details of the techniques the FBI used in its investigations, and I think I can make some fairly good guesses about the rest.

I assume that the responsible people at GTE were alarmed when they first realized what was happening. Because of their many and varied clients, and because their problem involved much more than a single state, Telemail must have called the FBI (whose agents, by the way, admitted more than once that they hoped to find more trouble than they did).

Next, the FBI must have told the customers not to send any important information over the mail system – or, perhaps, to move to a different mail service altogether during the investigation. After that, the agents started monitoring the mail and bulletins being sent by the hackers over Telemail. They used these messages as a source of clues to our real names and addresses, and to try to find out how criminal our intent was. I was told by two different FBI men that all the mail we sent was kept.

The FBI must have then taken the clues from our mail and used that information to locate a few of the people involved. From there, I would guess they obtained other names through long-distance phone records of calls placed by the hackers to their friends. After all this, the FBI had the names and addresses of about twenty people. Of those, they were most interested in members of the Inner Circle – either because the Inner Circle was the first to use the mail system or because we were the only organized hackers to use the system at all.

How It Ended

Several months after my initial meeting with the FBI agents, I was quite surprised to see all my confiscated computer equipment returned, via U.S. registered mail. Everything had been packed into a large cardboard box and protected with a little foam. Luckily, the damages were quite minor – under $200. I had a few friends whose equipment was completely useless when it was returned, but they were just happy to see it again at all.

Several months later, I was indicted. Once again, it took me by surprise. A reporter for a local newspaper called me in May 1984. He told me he had just read a wire story that said that I had been named in an indictment for three counts of wire fraud. I told him to call my lawyer, who was also surprised, but called me back with the news that I was, indeed, indicted on three counts of wire fraud by a federal grand jury in Alexandria, Virginia. According to the indictment:

> *"1. It was part of the device, scheme, and artifice to defraud that the defendant, William Landreth, would access the GTE Telenet Communications Corporation Electronic Mail Service through a telephone number located in San Diego, California.*

"2. It was further part of the device, scheme and artifice to defraud, that the defendant, William Landreth, would without GTE's authorization or the authorization of Raytheon Company or the American Hospital Supply Company [GTE customers], acquire user names and passwords or access codes...."

The indictment goes on to say that I created accounts so that unauthorized people could use the mail system.

After consulting with my attorney, I decided to plead guilty to the charges. The United States Attorneys agreed to drop two of the counts if I decided to plead guilty, leaving me with one count. Wire fraud is punishable by a prison term of not more than five years and/or a fine not exceeding $1000. Luckily, the prosecuting attorney was a reasonable person and agreed with a suggestion by my probation officer that I be fined $100 and be given 100 hours of community work to perform. Before sentencing me, however, the judge decided he wanted some psychological testing done on me – as he stated in court, "There's indication [Bill] has a very high IQ, but there's an indication he is not motivated to improve on that.... He's having trouble comparing right and wrong."

I was then sent to the Metropolitan Correctional Center in San Diego, and was given some IQ-type tests, ink-blot tests, personality tests, and a test to see how well I know my school subjects. I was not told how I did on the tests, but finished in two days and was out in four. Finally, on November 13, 1984, just over a year after I was caught, I was sentenced to three years' probation, during which I must complete my high-school education, go on to college or perform 200 hours of community service, and reimburse GTE $87 for unpaid telephone charges. I think the sentence is very fair, and I already know what my major will be....

ALL'S WELL   The main reason that my case even existed was that the people at Telemail did not know how to secure their system against unauthorized users. If they had, they would have kept us out. The fact that Telemail went directly to the FBI, and did not ask us if we would leave or if we could help them, makes me think that Telemail was very serious about security, but had no control over it.

This type of situation – a computer that needs security but does not have it – could be a very big problem, considering the fact that computers are becoming more and more a part of our lives every day.

I wrote this book because I think it is important that system owners, operators, and users have the knowledge to protect their systems from intruders. Now, I hope ignorance is no longer an excuse.

A Hacker's Evaluation Of Some Available Security Equipment

The information contained on the following pages is not meant to be taken as a technical review of computer-system security products, nor is it meant to suggest or recommend that you consider purchasing a particular unit.

I've included this appendix to give you a hacker's thoughts on some of the types of security equipment available to you before you commit yourself to any one. The list is *far* from complete, but it should help you decide what, exactly, you want from a security system, as well as what you should expect to get. Any of these units should help safeguard your computer system from outside access by a typical hacker. For pricing and more detailed information, please contact the companies themselves.

I also highly recommend that you investigate products you hear about other than those listed here. Once this appendix has given you an idea of what should be investigated, you will be better armed for such a process.

CALLBACK DEVICES

Sleuth *Manufacturer:* C.H. Systems, Inc., 8533 West Sunset Boulevard, Suite 106, Los Angeles, CA 90069, (213) 854-3536.

Type of device: Callback unit – designed to interface between a computer and a Hayes Smartmodem.

How it operates: The user connects with Sleuth after calling the remote computer, and Sleuth asks the caller for a name and password. After the name and password have been entered, the unit hangs up and verifies this information. If the name/password combination is found to be acceptable, the device calls the phone number corresponding to that name.

Advantages: The device is reasonably priced, and the name/password combination means that Sleuth is more of a filter and a callback than some other callback units are.

Disadvantages: There is a limit (74) of names/phone numbers per unit. Also, the device is designed for a limited situation, which is discussed next.

Best suited for: Sleuth is suited well to a small business with a small system – perhaps even a microcomputer. The limited number of authorized locations, and the fact that many larger systems have modems other than Hayes, makes Sleuth the type of device that is best for small businesses.

Comments: The company has just announced support for additional makes of modem; many other modems are Hayes-compatible, as well. The device can be used simply as a filter system, if desired, and there are a few unique features that are worth investigating if you think this device may help your security efforts.

Manufacturer: Digital Pathways, Inc., 1060 East Meadow Circle, Palo Alto, CA 94303, (415) 493-5034.

Type of device: Callback unit — using either your modem or theirs.

How it operates: The user calls the computer and enters his or her code on a touch-tone phone. The unit verifies the code, and tells the user, via a recorded voice, to expect callback. If all modems are busy, the voice tells the user there will be a delay before callback. The user can then decide not to be called back, or to accept the delay.

Advantages: The unit is flexible in design and has provisions for an extended log system.

Disadvantages: It is subject to the general problems for callback modems listed in Chapter 8, and the design, while flexible, may require more frequent maintenance than some other units.

Best suited for: Defender II seems well suited for most companies looking for callback unit security. Its design allows a company to start out with only a few outgoing lines and, over time, increase this number to hundreds, if needed.

Comments: This unit is quite user friendly, and should certainly be considered along with the other units available by anyone looking for a callback unit.

Manufacturer: Backus Data Systems, 1440 Koll Circle, Suite 110, San Jose, CA 95112, (408) 279-8711.

Type of device: Callback device — via RS-232 standard interface.

How it operates: In the basic system, the callback unit simply calls users back after asking for, and verifying, a six-character ID and a six-character password. There are many other options, however.

Advantages: Backus Data Systems is currently adding features and updating the system. The unit provides a versatile callback network.

Disadvantages: Because it is a system of several different devices, now being updated, possible weaknesses are impossible to pinpoint.

Best suited for: It is difficult to say who would gain the most benefit at this point. It does seem, however, that this system will not be targeted toward either the smallest or the largest of computer systems. I estimate that a system with from three to nine modem lines would find DialSafe most helpful.

Comments: Anyone who feels the need for callback security should certainly look into the DialSafe system, along with all the others mentioned here. By the time this is published, the DialSafe system should be well established and may very well be one of the better callback units available.

OZ/Guardian

Manufacturer: Tri-Data, 505 East Middlefield Road, Mountain View, CA 94039-7505, (415) 969-3700.

Type of device: Callback modem – RS-232 Bell 103/212a compatible.

How it operates: The user calls the modem and enters a password of 1 to 250 characters. The modem then hangs up, verifies the code, and calls the user back, if the password is valid.

Advantages: This system provides typical callback security, with up to 250 passwords/numbers for each unit. It also has provisions for limited audit trails.

Disadvantages: The unit is subject to the problems of most callback modems, as discussed in Chapter 8.

Best suited for: This is one of the callback modems that should be investigated by people who feel they require such a device. Companies that feel a callback modem would solve their security problems, will find the OZ/Guardian a very likely candidate.

Comments: The OZ/Guardian is a good callback unit. The support provided by Tri-Data makes the overall product better than some, but it is otherwise a typical representative of this group of devices.

Data Sentry

Manufacturer: Lockheed GETEX, 1100 Circle 75 Parkway N.W., Atlanta, GA 30339, (404) 951-0878.

Type of device: Callback modem. A Bell 212a- or 103-compatible modem that uses standard RS-232 ports.

How it operates: The user calls and leaves a phone number with the modem, which can be instructed either to call the given number or to check the number against a list of authorized phone numbers. After the modem calls the number, the user must provide a correct password or the modem will no longer call anyone at that number.

Advantages: The device can be programmed to call back *any* number given to it, without regard to lists of authorized numbers, and it maintains a list of unauthorized, as well as authorized, numbers.

Disadvantages: There is a limited number of both authorized and unauthorized numbers, and the device itself is subject to most of the problems discussed under callback modems in Chapter 8.

Best suited for: This device is best for a high-security computer system, because it may cut off authorized users who type their passwords incorrectly. It also has a somewhat limited authorized-number list, so it is a bit restricted, unless the number of users who may access the computer via modem is small – as in high-security situations.

Comments: As with most external security devices, the Data Sentry System is not likely to be cracked by a typical hacker. This system, however, like many others available, does not provide security against a hacker who has access to any directly connected terminal or to the computer itself.

Manufacturer: LeeMAH Datacom Security Systems, 3948 Trust Way, Hayward, CA 94545, (415) 786-0790.

Secure Access Multiport (SAM)

Type of device: Callback unit – SAM is placed between your modems and the phone lines.

How it operates: The user calls in and enters a one- to fifteen-digit Location Identification Number (LIN). If the LIN is valid, an acknowledgment tone is emitted so the user will know to expect callback within five to ten seconds.

Advantages: The SAM can handle more callback locations – over 2300 – than any other I have seen. It also has quite a bit of support in the way of an extended log system, as well as such features as "Time Portals," which restrict certain LINs from operating during certain time periods.

Disadvantages: The general problems discussed under callback modems in Chapter 8.

Best suited for: Anyone who needs a callback unit should consider the SAM. Its large size makes it best suited for larger systems, but its price is very reasonable, and LeeMAH will customize a unit to certain specifications to minimize cost.

Comments: The Secure Access Multiport is a typical callback unit, with above-average support from the parent company and a reasonable price. It is also quite versatile in terms of potential expansion.

FILTER DEVICES

ComputerSentry

Manufacturer: TACT Technology, 100 North 20th Street, Philadelphia, PA 19103, (800) 523-0103.

Type of device: A filter unit which is placed between a modem and a phone line.

How it operates: The user calls and a synthesized voice asks for an ID code, which can be entered either by touch tone or by voice. As soon as the user enters a correct code, the modem-to-modem connection is allowed.

Advantages: The unit allows a selectable number of false attempts, after which an alarm can be set to go off. The device is very friendly to authorized users.

Disadvantages: Some users may have difficulty in using auto-dial modems with this particular device. Unauthorized users who gain access also find the unit user friendly.

Best suited for: This filter system could probably be used by a company that is not quite certain whether to invest in a callback unit or to stay with basic password security. The device offers a good compromise level of security for many people.

Comments: A typical filter system, with better-than-average provisions for handling unauthorized code entries. The synthesized voice and a provision for allowing the user to enter the code verbally are also unique features.

Manufacturer: Sutton Designs, Inc., 111 South Cayuga, Suite 200, Ithaca, NY 14850, (607) 277-4301.

EnterCept

Type of device: Filter system—one per RS-232 modem.

How it operates: The user calls the system and enters a six-character password. Each character can be any of the 128 ASCII characters. If the correct password is given, the user is then allowed to communicate with the host computer, which will probably also have its own password procedure.

Advantages: This product provides a multi-level password system and is an inexpensive guard against casual hackers.

Disadvantages: It is subject to the same weaknesses of *all* password systems, and is generally not useful for local terminals or for computers on public networks.

Best suited for: This system is best for a typical non-classified computer installment that has had trouble in keeping hackers off its system. In addition, the owner of a system with too many users who are too lax about security should, in general, find this type of device the next logical step in enhancing security.

Comments: This device is not intended to be a security cure-all, but what it does—cut the number of hackers on a typical system to zero—it does very well. In most cases, this type of device is actually *more* effective against hackers than a callback unit. Hackers have other procedures they can use against callback units; against this type of unit, they must crack the password or forget about getting into the system altogether.

ENCRYPTION DEVICES

Sherlock Information Security System

Manufacturer: Analytics Communications Systems, 1820 Michael Faraday Drive, Reston, VA 22090, (703) 471-0892.

Type of device: DES (Data Encryption Standard) Encryption. Each terminal is supplied with an Information Security Module (ISM) which is responsible for encrypting and decrypting data.

How it operates: The central unit generates DES encryption keys, which are then used to encrypt and decrypt data. In the case of remote terminals, DES keys are transported by way of the "Authenti-Key" device, which is a solid-state "key" containing the encryption code.

Advantages: Data encrypted with this method will NOT be decrypted without the correct key or the effort and resources of a full-scale corporate or governmental effort – and even then, the probability of success is not that great. In addition, keys are generated by the machine, which is programmed to choose complex keys; the result is not known to any human being.

Disadvantages: In many cases, the DES key will need to be transported. Since it is an actual, solid device, the key can be stolen like anything else. Some people also attack the Data Encryption Standard itself, saying it can already be decoded by government agencies. But this opinion has never been confirmed, and many people say that it is 100 percent untrue.

Best suited for: This is a device that is best suited for a very high-security situation. It is a very comprehensive, well-implemented system, but the cost per user, in addition to a little bit of inconvenience, makes it most useful for a very high-level security installation.

Comments: The company that produces the Information Security System has fifteen years of experience in communications security, working with such institutions as the U.S. Department of Defense. The company maintains that all possible encryption techniques were scrutinized before this particular procedure was chosen.

Manufacturer: Obsidian Computer Systems, 236 North Santa Cruz Avenue, Suite 243, Los Gatos, CA 95030, (408) 395-7900.

Super Encryptor II

Type of device: Software encryption – a program for MS-DOS or CP/M microcomputers.

How it operates: After the user calls up the encryption program, he or she enters the key or keys. The file is encrypted, and the old file is overwritten on the disk by the new file. If the file has already been encrypted with the same key, the encryption process will actually decrypt the file.

Advantages: It is probably impossible for a hacker to decrypt a file encrypted with the Super Encryptor II. The encryption technique is fairly quick, although larger files may still take time to encrypt.

Disadvantages: The user must choose long and complex keys...and remember them. The product is also subject to the general problems of software encryption discussed in Chapter 8.

Best suited for: People who use a microcomputer to obtain security-sensitive data from larger systems may have a need to encrypt this data. Also, some people may have a need to encrypt data from a microcomputer so that it can be safely transported from one location to another, with the key being transported by another method.

Comments: Encryption of this type is unlikely to be used on an everyday basis, unless the effort involved is really necessary.

UNIQUE IDs

Manufacturer: Avant-Garde Computing, Inc., 8000 Commerce Parkway, Mt. Laurel, NJ 08054, (609) 778-7000.

Net/Guard System

Type of device: Multi-purpose network security.

How it operates: The Net/Guard system should be transparent to users. In those cases in which the owner of the system chooses to have Net/Guard perform callback or filter functions, however, the system will act as a typical callback or filter device.

Advantages: This device provides an operator with instant, up-to-date information on network usage. It also allows the operator to restrict the use of specific accounts to certain days of the week, certain hours of the day, or certain parts of the network or computer.

Disadvantages: This is a major device, best integrated into a new system. It is also designed for larger systems, so it is too expensive and comprehensive for many systems.

Best suited for: It is best suited for large systems with large security concerns...a system that is best used with an operator always on duty.

Comments: The Net/Guard system, when used where it is needed, as it is designed to be used, can be one of the most comprehensive and effective security systems available. Security, however, is only one of the functions that Net/Guard performs, so a buyer interested in security alone may pay for other, non-required, advantages. It should be looked into, however, if your system warrants such protection.

Data Lock & Key *Manufacturer:* MicroFrame, Inc., 205 University Avenue, New Brunswick, NJ 08901, (201) 828-4499.

Type of device: Unique ID—One unit with every user, main unit at the main computer.

How it operates: The user calls in with his or her data key, which is a box about the size of a small modem, and connects with the computer. The computer may or may not have further password security, but no one without a valid data key will be connected at all.

Advantages: The physical lock and key on the Data Lock & Key prevents misuse, and the system offers provisions for extended logs.

Disadvantages: There is the possibility of a stolen unit gaining entry, and this device may possibly lead to laziness in terms of local security.

Best suited for: The Data Lock & Key seems best suited for a smaller-than-average computer installation, with above-average security requirements. It will certainly keep out the hackers, though I don't know if it was designed with thieves in mind.

Comments: While the Data Lock & Key does a good job of making the user do as little as possible, the user is an active part of the process. This may be good or bad, depending on your viewpoint, but this fact suggests to me that the unit is designed with a high-security situation in mind. I should also mention that the Data Lock & Key has excellent procedures for handling lost or stolen keys that are *reported.*

Index

E

Electronic mail, 189-90
Encryption, 144-48
    problems with, 147-48
    Sherlock Information Security System, 222-23
    Super Encryptor II, 223
Engressia, Joe, 29-31
External security devices, 143-60
    nonstandard, 157-58

F

Files
    added, 188
    altered, 187
    directories, 188
    in electronic mail, 189
    prior versions, 189
Filter systems, 153-54
    ComputerSentry, 220-21
    EnterCept, 221-22
Fingerprint verification, 159
Floppy disks
    and security, 165-67
414s, 35-36

G

General Telephone (GTE), 10

H

Hackers, 25-26
    confronting, 201-2
    discouraging, 114-16
    of the eighties, 34-36
    enlisting, 203
    handling, 195-96
    hierarchy of, 51
    identifying, 200-201
    goals, 75
    levels of hacking, 69-72
    methods used by, 76
        database hack, 83

Hackers, methods used by *(continued)*
    decoy, 83-87
    hack-hack, 81-82
    logic bombs, 97-100
    remote sysop, 90-92
    reverse hack, 82-83
    short hack, 82
    trapdoor, 92-94
    Trojan horse, 94-97
    worm programs, 100-102
    motivation of, 58-59
    neutralizing, 205
    profiles of, 59-69
        the Crasher, 66-68
        the Novice, 61-62
        the Student, 62-64, 197
        the Thief, 68-69
        the Tourist, 64-66
    removing, 206
    "rights" of, 51
    rules of, 60
    of the seventies, 28-34
    of the sixties, 26-28
    telltale signs, 185-94
    thinking like, 197-98
Help, 52-56
    inside a company, 125

I

IBM-370, 78
Information networks, 34-35, 104-5
Information trading, 14-15
Inner Circle, 16-23
    capers, 19-23
    "code of ethics," 18-19
    formation of, 16-19
    Inner Circle Seven, 18

L

LISP, 27
Log systems, 154-56
    improved, 154-56
    logging on, 133-37, 186-87
    logic bombs, 97-100
    problems with, 155-56

M

N

O

P

R

S

T

U

V

W

*The manuscript for this book was prepared and submitted
to Microsoft Press in electronic form. Text files were
processed and formatted using Microsoft Word.*

Cover design by Greg Hickman
Cover illustration by David Shannon
Interior text design by Chris Stern

*Text composition by Microsoft Press in Rotation with
display in Erbar, using CCI Book and the Mergenthaler
Linotron 202 digital phototypesetter.*

Other Titles Available from Tempus Books

COMPUTER LIB/DREAM MACHINES
Ted Nelson

"An exuberant, multifont compendium of computing proverbs, anecdotes, jokes, predictions, and politics. Still as fresh and relevant as it was a dozen years ago, Computer Lib is a browser's gold mine."   PC World

Originally published in 1974, COMPUTER LIB/DREAM MACHINES provided inspiration to today's industry greats. Nelson anticipated the personal computer revolution, made outlandish predictions (many of which have proven true), and expounded on his vision of nonsequential data storage — something he dubbed hypertext. Long unavailable, COMPUTER LIB has been updated with new commentaries and insights from Nelson.

336 pages, 9¼ x 9¾, softcover, $18.95   [Order Code 0-914845-49-7]

PROGRAMMERS AT WORK, revised
Susan Lammers

"PROGRAMMERS AT WORK…provides comfort, inspiration and a sense of community with those who have already succeeded in the field…it is not to be missed."   The New York Times

A collection of captivating interviews that probe the minds of nineteen of today's most notable programmers. The interviews highlight the forces, the events, and the personality traits that influenced Andy Hertzfeld (Macintosh Operating System), John Warnock (PostScript), C. Wayne Ratliff (dBASE), Jonathan Sachs (Lotus 1-2-3), Bill Gates (BASIC), and many others. A lively appendix provides some actual code and worksheets from these software wizards.

400 pages, 6 x 9, softcover, $9.95   [Order Code 1-55615-211-6]

MACHINERY OF THE MIND
George Johnson

Reporting from the frontiers of artificial intelligence (AI), Johnson introduces the masters of AI — Minsky, Schank, Feigenbaum, and others — and explores the work being done on machines that understand English, discover scientific theories on their own, and create original works of art and music. MACHINERY OF THE MIND is a compelling introduction to AI programs and to their designers.

352 pages, 6⅛ x 9, softcover, $9.95   [Order Code 1-55615-010-5]

THE TOMORROW MAKERS
Grant Fjermedal

"This nonfiction book has enough new ideas for 16 Star Trek sequels. And better dialogue."   Rudy Rucker

A spellbinding account of visionary scientists and their modern-day quest for immortality. Award-winning author Fjermedal details the astounding work being done today in robotics and artificial intelligence on organic molecular computers smaller than a grain of sand, on lifelike androids that are intelligent and charming, and — most extraordinary of all — on the process of downloading human minds into computerized robots that will live forever.

288 pages, 6⅛ x 9, softcover, $8.95   [Order Code 1-55615-113-6]

THE NEW WIZARD WAR
Robyn Shotwell Metcalfe

A riveting and timely report on the legal and illegal transfer of high technology from the U.S. to the U.S.S.R. Metcalfe expertly probes the issues: the loss of U.S. technological leadership, the question of national security, the wisdom of U.S.–Soviet scientific cooperation, the Gorbachev agenda, and the balance between government and private control over the flow of technology. The case studies in THE NEW WIZARD WAR — mixing international intrigue, military secrets, million-dollar payoffs, and bureaucratic snafus — provide an eye-opening, firsthand look at the Soviets' successful methods of acquiring Western technology.

288 pages, 6 x 9, hardcover, $17.95   [Order Code 1-55615-016-4]